# PUZZLE QUEST

## The missing astronaut

Written & illustrated
by Kia Marie Hunt

Published by Collins
An imprint of HarperCollins Publishers
HarperCollins Publishers
Westerhill Road
Bishopbriggs
Glasgow G64 2QT

www.harpercollins.co.uk

HarperCollins Publishers
1st Floor, Watermarque Building
Ringsend Road
Dublin 4, Ireland

10 9 8 7 6 5 4 3 2

ISBN 978-0-00-845747-1

Printed and bound in the UK using 100% renewable electricity
at CPI Group (UK) Ltd

Publisher: Michelle I'Anson
Author and illustrator: Kia Marie Hunt
Project Manager: Sarah Woods
Designer: Kevin Robbins

# PUZZLE
# QUEST

## The missing astronaut

 Written & illustrated
by Kia Marie Hunt

It's all over the news.

The world's most famous astronaut has gone missing in outer space!

Everyone read the newspaper story about it... but not everyone noticed the secret message that you decoded:

GOOD AT PUZZLES? CRACKING CODES, SOLVING MYSTERIES?

WANT TO EXPLORE THE UNIVERSE?

IF SO, WE NEED YOU!

YOU CAN JOIN THE SPACE ACADEMY TODAY AND HELP US LOOK FOR

THE MISSING ASTRONAUT...

Well, you have to admit that does sound like fun...

It's time to go on an adventure!

Attend the Space Academy then launch into space on your mission to find the astronaut. Be ready to solve more than 100 interplanetary puzzles, collecting lots of cosmic clues along the way!

Things you'll need:

★ **This book**
★ **A pen or pencil**
★ **Your amazing brain**

That's it!

**Will YOU take on the quest?**

**Psssst!
Always look out for
this hand symbol:**

This means you've found a clue.

Write down all the clues you find in your Clue Logbooks
(on pages **30, 54, 78, 102** and **126!**)

EARTH!

# OUR SOLAR SYSTEM

PLANET PEDRA 202
(6 light years away!)

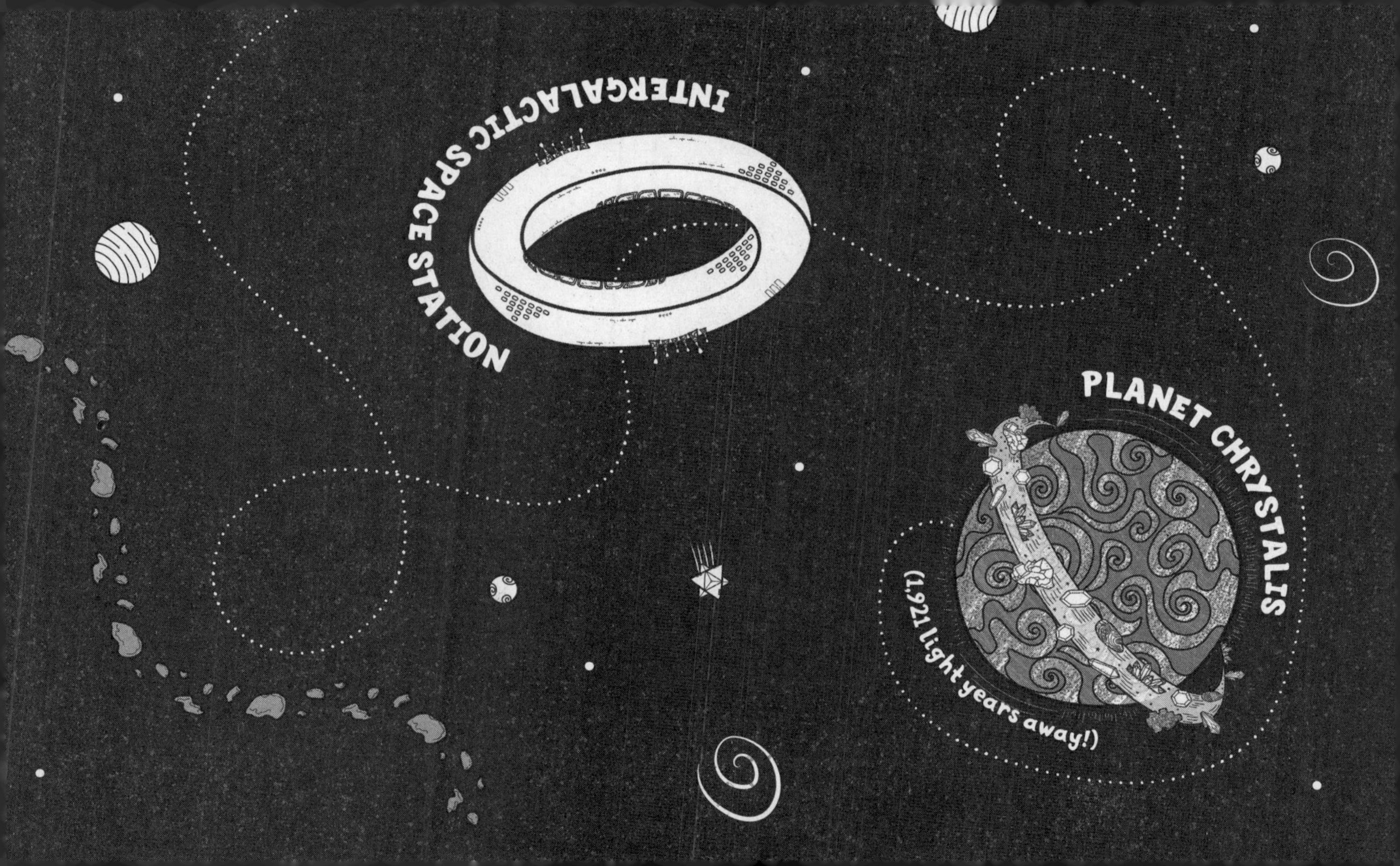

PLANET CHRYSTALIS

(1,921 light years away!)

INTERGALACTIC SPACE STATION

Before you blast off to search space for the missing astronaut, you'll need to learn how to become an astronaut yourself!

That's right, it's time for **SPACE TRAINING** So, get ready for some gravity games, space food fun and countdown challenges!

# Let's start with some training puzzles!

Follow the lines and write the letter from each circle in the space at the end of each line to reveal a new word. Some letters have already been done for you.

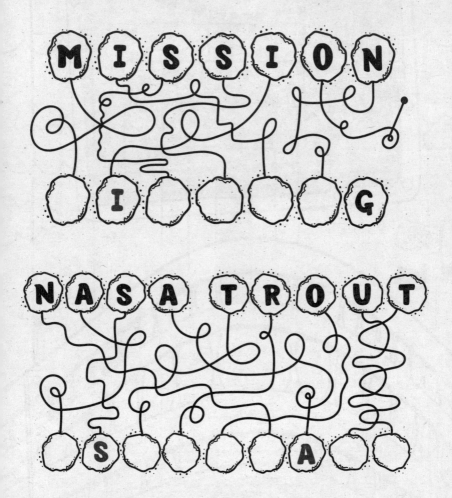

Can you find your way from Training Room 1, all the way through the maze to get to Training Room 2?

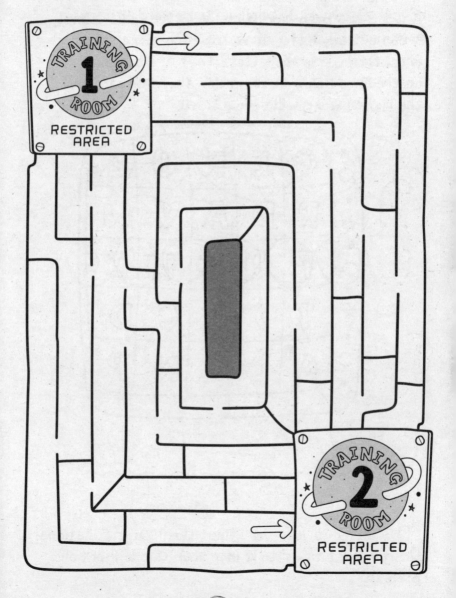

Can you guess what kind of training you'll be doing in this room? Solve the puzzle below to find out.

A word has been hidden in the letter grid. Simply cross out any letter that appears more than once, then write the letters that are left over on the lines below in the order they appear, and the hidden word will reveal itself.

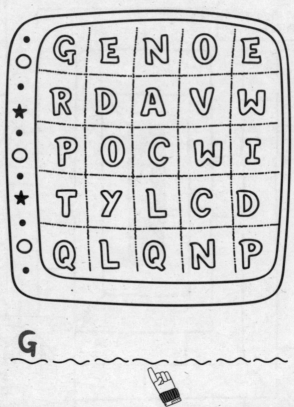

G _ _ _ _ _ _ _

(This letter is your very first clue, congratulations! Don't forget to write it into your clue logbook on page 30!)

Solve these puzzles to test the G-force simulators.

Start with the number at the top, above 'start'. Then follow the maths instructions in turn around the wheel until you reach the top again. Try it in an anti-clockwise direction, then do it clockwise to find out which way gives you the answer in the middle.

Hint: in this example, start with 2 at the top then, if you go in an anti-clockwise direction, the answer is 6.

If you go in a clockwise direction, the answer is 8. This matches the number in the middle, so clockwise is the correct answer!

clockwise

To get prepared for being in space, you must train in a room that has zero gravity. Without gravity, the letters in the words below are floating away!

**Unscramble the letters to reveal the correct words.**

(Hint: they are all names of things found in our solar system.)

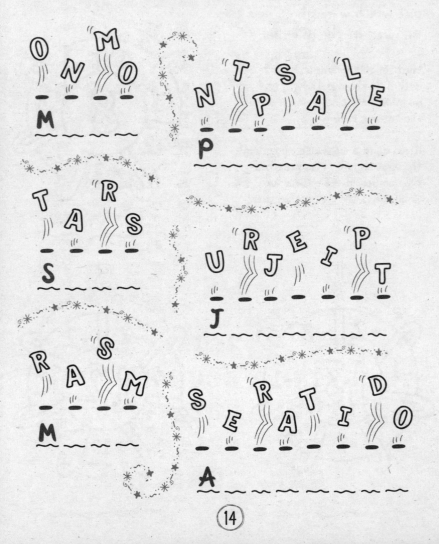

O N M O

M _ _ _ _

N T S P A L E

P _ _ _ _ _ _

T A R S S

S _ _ _ _

U R J E I P T

J _ _ _ _ _ _

R A S M M

M _ _ _ _

S E R A T I D O

A _ _ _ _ _ _ _ _

There are lots of fun tricks you can do while in zero gravity!

Can you find all ten words in the wordsearch below? Words may be hidden horizontally or vertically.

```
B A C K F L I P K X
S O M E R S A U L T
A X R N X G L I D E
E A O Y S U N F D S
L U L X B D D L I P
D D L E A P R O H I
F B O U N C E A Q N
L R V T W I S T S I
Y K E R F L M A T A
S S R A H E C T R U
```

FLY        TWIST
SPIN       BOUNCE
LEAP       BACKFLIP
GLIDE      ROLL OVER
FLOAT      SOMERSAULT

Can you spot the five differences between these two pictures of the Zero Gravity Training Room?

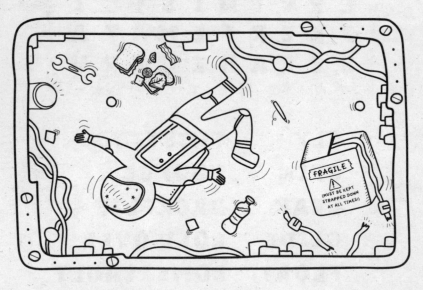

Lots of things are floating around the room because there's no gravity to hold them down.

Which silhouettes correctly match each floating object? Circle your answers.

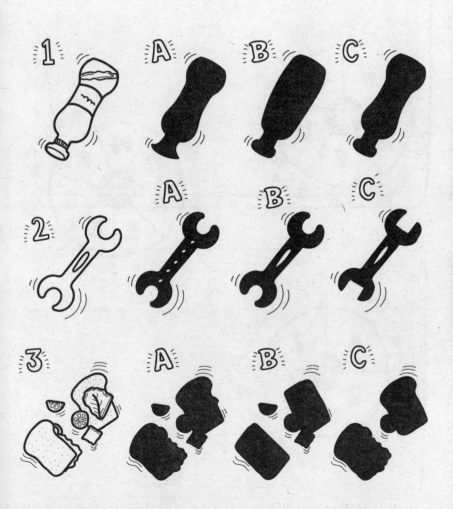

As an astronaut you'll eat all kinds of weird and wonderful space food.

In the word-wheels, find the names of three foods. Each word starts with the centre letter and uses all the letters in the wheel once.

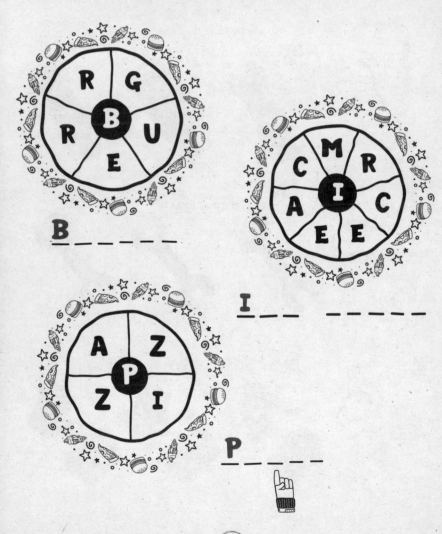

B _ _ _ _ _

I _ _   _ _ _ _ _

P _ _ _ _

Below are two jumbled up space menus.

Unscramble the letters to find out what's inside each tin, box or packet. Some letters have already been done for you.

## Space Menu 1

## Space Menu 2

### Starters

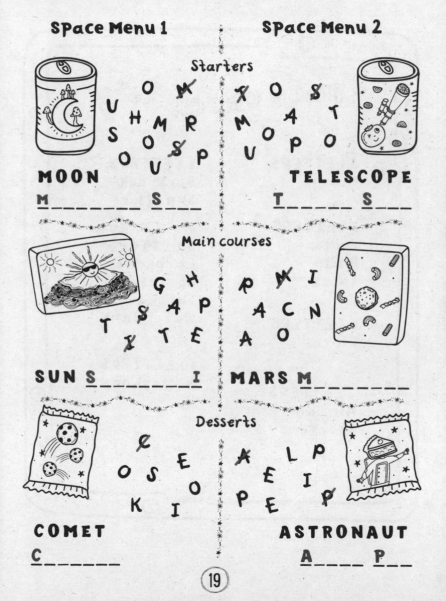

**MOON**

M _ _ _ _ _ _ _ S _ _ _

**TELESCOPE**

T _ _ _ _ _ S _ _ _

### Main courses

**SUN** S _ _ _ _ _ _ _ _ I

**MARS** M _ _ _ _ _ _ _

### Desserts

**COMET**

C _ _ _ _ _ _

**ASTRONAUT**

A _ _ _ P _ _

Now you're trained up and your space food is ready, it's time to start preparing your kit. As an astronaut you have a long checklist of things you need to take with you.

## space checklist! ✓

**3 LETTERS**
Cap

**5 LETTERS**
Boots
Radio
Tubes

**6 LETTERS**
Gloves

**7 LETTERS**
Air tank
Speaker

**8 LETTERS**
Backpack
Sun visor

**9 LETTERS**
Earphones
Spacesuit
Sunshades
Water tank

**10 LETTERS**
Microphone

Place each of the words, from the checklist on the opposite page, into the empty squares to create a filled crossword grid. Each word is used once so cross it off the list as you place it to help you keep track.

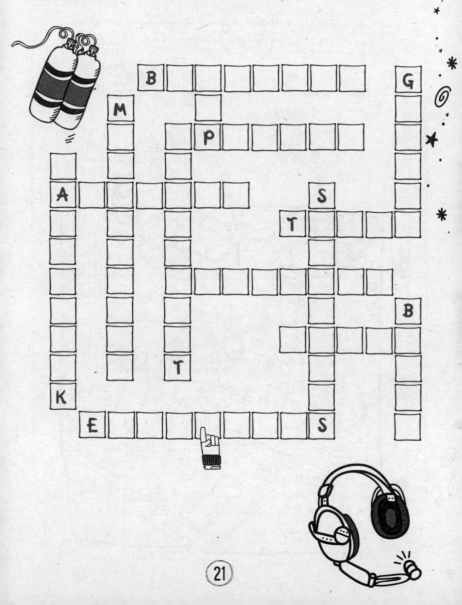

# What a mess!

Can you find the items below in the grid? When you've found each item write the grid reference next to it. One has been done for you.

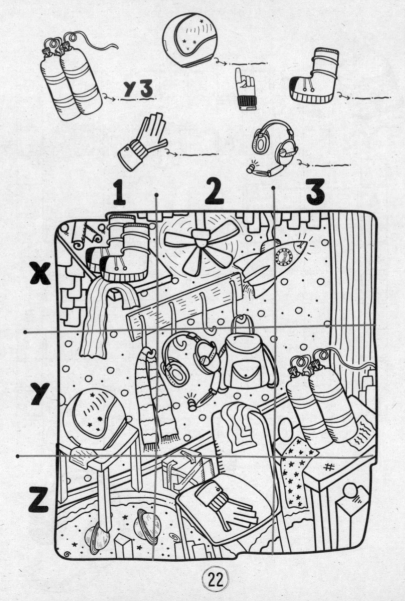

Y3

Now you've got a space suit and found all your equipment, you just need to organise your space socks!

You can move up, down or sideways, but you can't move diagonally and you must follow the socks in this order:

Use the code Key below to crack the code and reveal what part of your training is next. Some letters have already been done for you.

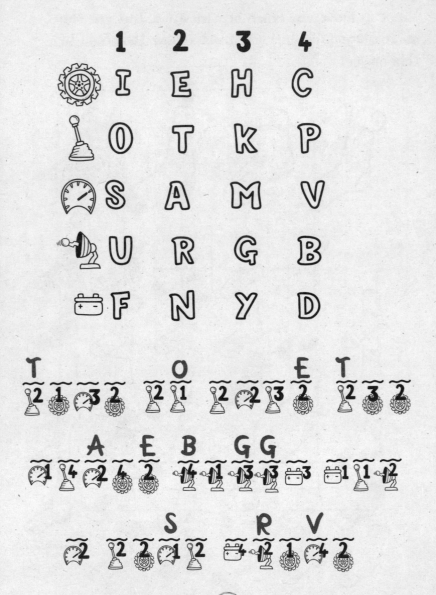

Drive the space buggy through the maze from start to finish!

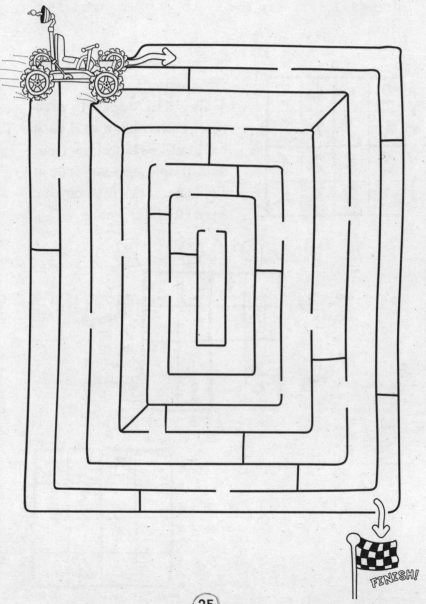

FINISH!

As part of your space training, you need to learn basic level Rocket Mechanics, which means knowing your numbers! Practise working with numbers by solving the space sudoku puzzles below.

| 2 | 1 | 4 | 3 |
|---|---|---|---|
| 4 | 3 | 1 | 2 |
| 3 | 4 | 2 | 1 |
| 1 | 2 | 3 | 4 |

In the sudoku grids below, the numbers 1, 2, 3 and 4 should be added to each row, each column and each 2x2 bold outlined box, but should only appear once in each one. The first one has been done for you.

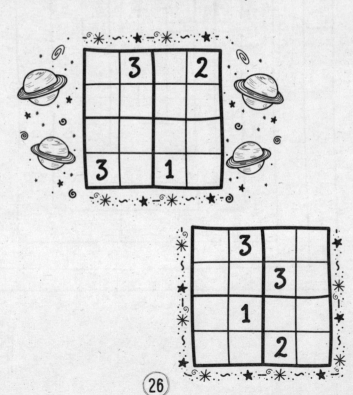

On your space mission, you'll pick up signals from different planets, and you might need to use your awesome skills to crack number codes.

Solve the number problem below each letter in the Key. Then use the answers to fill in the spaces below to reveal the message. Some letters have been done for you.

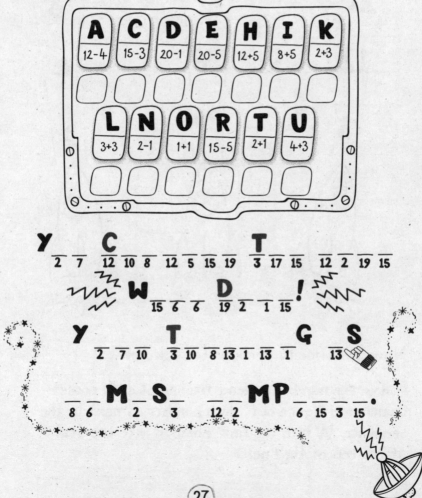

| A | C | D | E | H | I | K |
|---|---|---|---|---|---|---|
| 12-4 | 15-3 | 20-1 | 20-5 | 12+5 | 8+5 | 2+3 |

| L | N | O | R | T | U |
|---|---|---|---|---|---|
| 3+3 | 2-1 | 1+1 | 15-5 | 2+1 | 4+3 |

Y __  C __ __  __ __ __ __  T __ __  __ __ __ __
2  7   12  10  8   12  5  15  19   3  17  15   12  2  19  15

W __ __   D __ __ __ !
15  6  6   19  2  1  15

Y __ __   T __ __ __ __ __ __   G __ S __
2  7  10   3  10  8  13  1  13  1   13

__ __ M __ S __   __ __ MP __ __ __ __ .
8  6   2   3   12  2   6  15  3  15

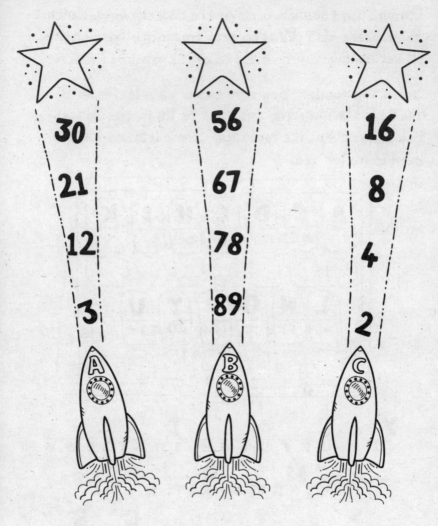

30
21
12
3
A

56
67
78
89
B

16
8
4
2
C

Now, it's time to prepare for take-off...

Follow the numbers along the line of each rocket launch and figure out which number is next in the sequence. Write the final number into the star at the top of the line.

Can you find these words in the rocket wordsearch as you take off? Words may be hidden horizontally or vertically.

COUNTDOWN

THREE

TWO

ONE

LIFTOFF

LAUNCH

BLAST

SUPERSPEED

R
U T K
T S H O I
Y W H R I A G
U O N E G U P
S T Q R E K Z P F
Y L B L A S T O N
M R G O A I S C E Q S
S L A U N C H H Z U J
I U I C C O Q F S X W F
B F F W P B P A A X I U
W Z M L I F T O F F A F B L
M E A O Q P C M L J W Q H P E
B F S U P E R S P E E D L R Z M
M I J C O U N T D O W N B N A Z
H G X J Q Z I K T L K D O X W I S
K G                         I N

# CLUE LOGBOOK: SPACE TRAINING

Congratulations, you have completed space training!

As you hurtle through space towards your first destination, take a minute to record any clues you have found so far.

Remember, clues are pointed out by this symbol:

Write the clue letter next to the page number where you found it:

Page: 12     Clue letter: ◯

Page: 18     Clue letter: ◯

Page: 21     Clue letter: ◯

Page: 22     Clue letter: ◯

Page: 27     Clue letter: ◯

(Blank 'notes' pages like this are handy for jotting down any notes or working out when you're busy solving puzzles!

You could also use them to write, doodle, or for anything else you like while on your space quest!)

....*~~~~

# First stop:
# PLANET PEDRA 202

This planet was the last known location of the astronaut before going missing.

Are you ready to solve plenty of magma mind games, crater conundrums and moon mysteries on this volcanic planet?

Clue Logbook for this chapter is on Page 54!

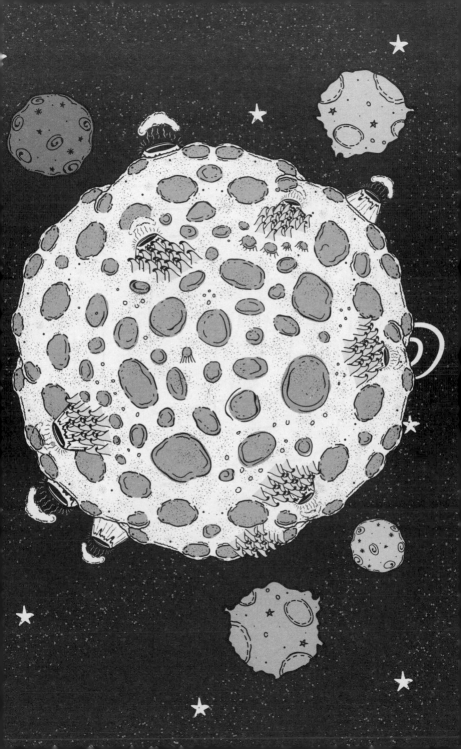

Can you guide your spacecraft through the maze to safely land on target on Planet Pedra 202?

As you set foot on this strange new planet, you discover lots of weird and wonderful trees, mountains, and even some footprints!

**Which silhouette correctly matches each new discovery? Circle your answers.**

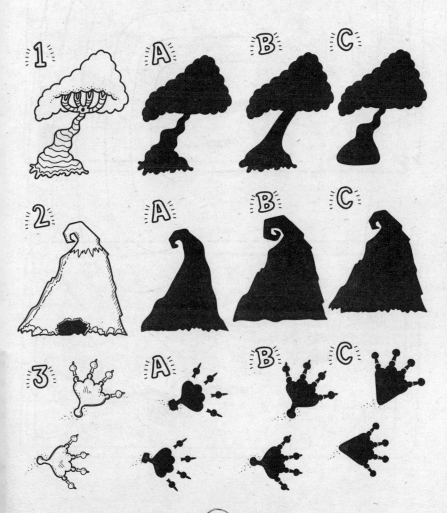

Can you spot the six differences between these two pictures of your view on Planet Pedra 202?

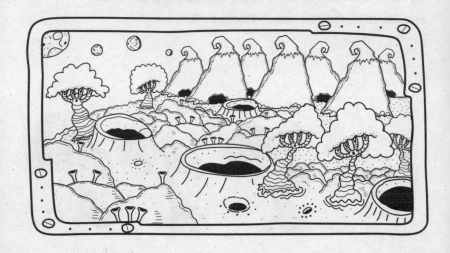

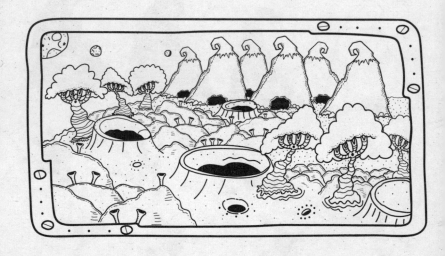

You notice many funny-looking antennae poking up from behind the rocks. Then they start to move! Perhaps you should follow them...

**Which of the tangled paths below leads to the antennae? Write your answer in the box.**

F G H I J K L

You follow the moving antennae all the way to a cluster of hot springs. You've never seen anything like this before, hot water and steam is shooting up from the ground right up into the sky!

Follow the numbers up through the steam of each hot spring and figure out which number is next in the sequence. Write the final number into the big cloud of steam at the top of each spring.

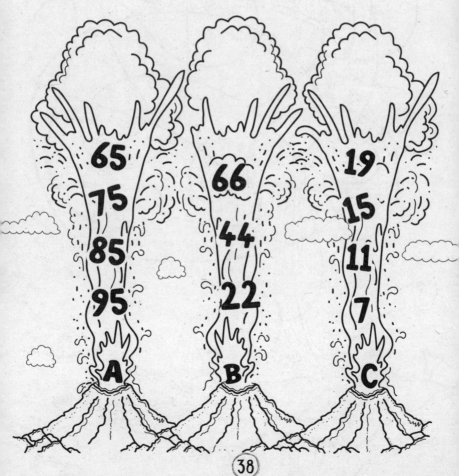

A: 65, 75, 85, 95

B: 66, 44, 22

C: 19, 15, 11, 7

Next, you follow the antennae across one of the highest bridges you've ever seen, right over a huge waterfall of rushing hot water.

Scribble out every other letter. Write the letters that are left over on the lines below. This will reveal a message. The first letter has been done for you.

D _ _ ' _ _ _ _ _ _ _ _ !

Wow! You follow the antennae through lots of impressive places filled with all kinds of volcanoes.

Can you find the names of all seven places you see (below) in the wordsearch on the opposite page? Words may be hidden in the grid horizontally or vertically.

ASH TOWERS

CINDER CLIFFS

CONE COLUMNS

FIRE ARCHES

LAVA CAVES

LAVA LAKE

MAGMA TUNNEL

```
C O N E C O L U M N S F
J L U J I W T A G A M P
P S O O N Z W S L L A F
R I J X D X T H A T G I
U L D B E M A T V P M R
R O F H R I X O A J A E
S I N R C O Z W C S T A
L A V A L A K E A E U R
A S N T I Q W R V Y N C
T T V I F N L S E T N H
S S R A F Q P D S Y E E
W R L B S X S S G I L S
```

In the sudoku grids below, the numbers 1, 2, 3 and 4 should be added to each row, each column and each 2x2 bold outlined box, but should only appear once in each one. The first one has been done for you.

| 3 | 4 | 1 | 2 |
| 1 | 2 | 3 | 4 |
| 4 | 3 | 2 | 1 |
| 2 | 1 | 4 | 3 |

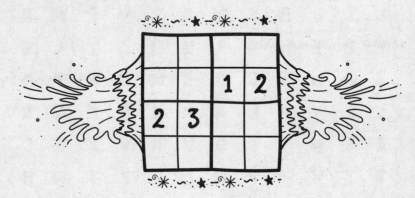

You come to some fields of jagged spikes, but they look dangerous!

To work out the danger level of each spikey field, scribble out any odd numbers, then add up all of the even numbers in the rocks and write the totals into the warning signs. The first one has been done for you.

You need to cross the least dangerous spikey field. Which one has the lowest danger total?

On the other side of the jagged spikey fields,
you finally catch up to the antennae...

...only to discover that they belong to some
very funny-looking aliens!

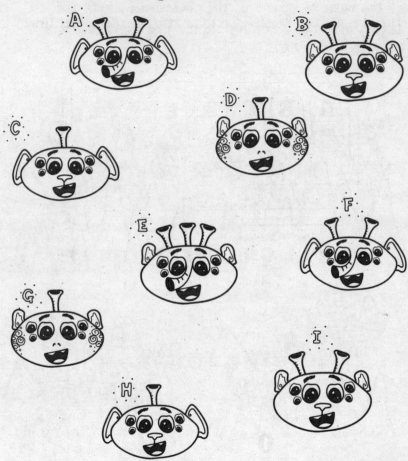

Odd one out: which of the curious aliens
above does not have a matching twin?
Look closely at their antennae, ears
and weird little noses.

You tell the aliens about your mission, and guess what? They saw the missing astronaut!

They'll tell you everything, but only if you help them with something first...

Use the symbol key below to crack the code and find out what the aliens want.

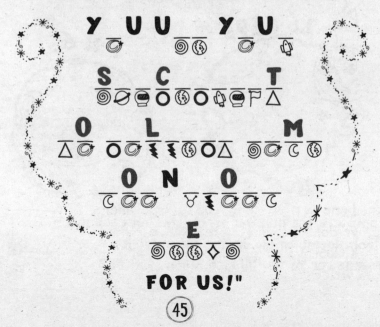

**"WE'LL ONLY HELP YOU IF:**

**FOR US!"**

Moonblooms are plants that used to grow all over Planet Pedra.

But, ever since a cosmic storm burnt them all away, the only moonblooms left are on just one of Planet Pedra's four moons!

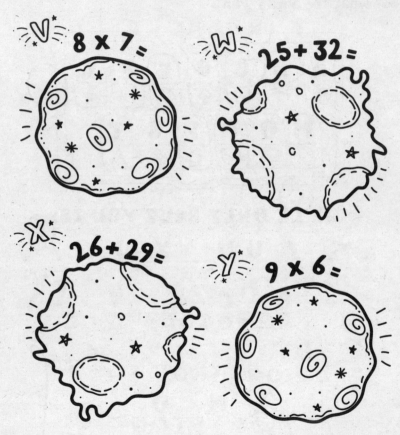

V* 8 x 7 =

W* 25 + 32 =

X* 26 + 29 =

Y* 9 x 6 =

Complete the number problems on each moon. Moonblooms grow on the moon with an answer of 55. Which moon is that?

Follow the lines and write the letter from each circle in the space at the end of each line to reveal the lunar-themed words. Some letters have already been done for you.

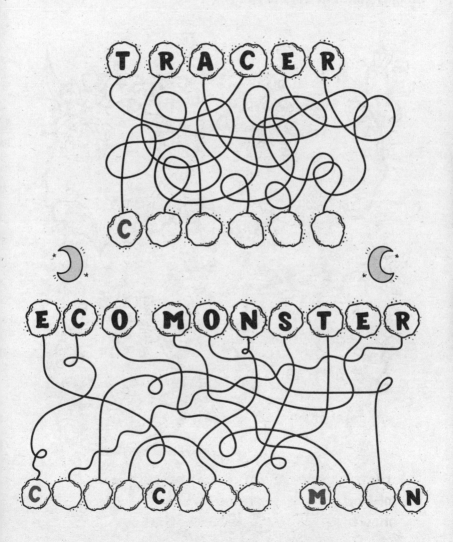

On this moon, you must collect seeds from all four kinds of moonbloom.

You can move up, down or sideways, but you can't move diagonally and you must follow the moonblooms in this order:

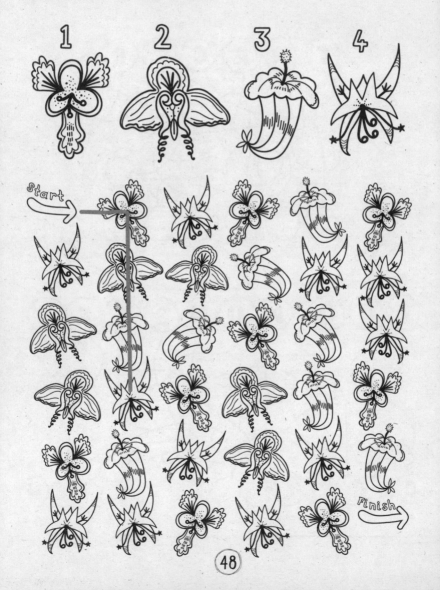

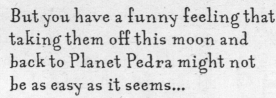

You have collected all the moonbloom seeds you need. Great!

But you have a funny feeling that taking them off this moon and back to Planet Pedra might not be as easy as it seems...

See if you are right by finding the hidden word in the letter grid below.

Simply cross out any letter that appears more than once and the hidden word will reveal itself. Write the word on the line at the bottom of the page.

| H | T | L | T | D |
| B | U | Z | X | L |
| V | A | N | X | B |
| L | O | H | G | O |
| U | Z | E | R | V |

_____

# Uh oh!

Before you can leave this moon and take the moonbloom seeds you collected back to the aliens, you'll have to get away from this angry Moonbear!

**Can you find your way through the maze so you can escape?**

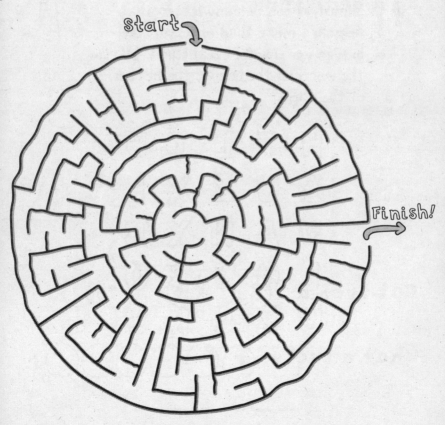

start

Finish!

What happens next? Complete the puzzle below to find out!

Follow the lines and write the letter from each circle in the space at the end of each line.

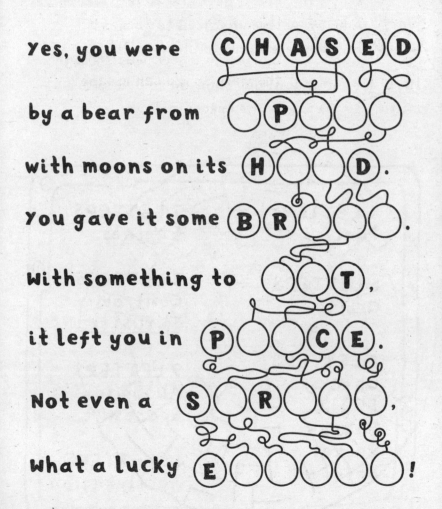

Yes, you were (C)(H)(A)(S)(E)(D)

by a bear from ( )(P)( )( )

with moons on its (H)( )(D).

You gave it some (B)(R)( )( )( ).

With something to ( )( )(T),

it left you in (P)( )( )(C)(E).

Not even a (S)( )(R)( ),

what a lucky (E)( )( )( )( )!

The aliens are very pleased with the moonbloom seeds you brought back for them! They reward you with some very important information: the missing astronaut left Planet Pedra and took off for Planet Chrystalis.

Now you know where you need to go next, let's follow the astronaut to Chrystalis!

It's a very long journey though, so you take a minute to prepare your spacecraft...

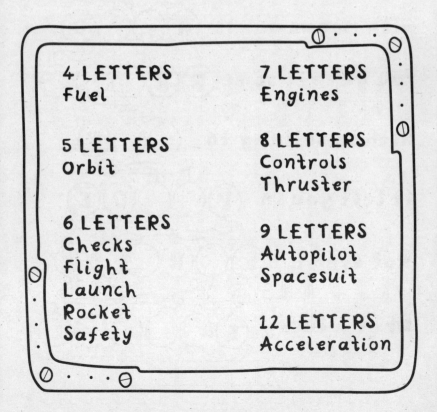

**4 LETTERS**
Fuel

**5 LETTERS**
Orbit

**6 LETTERS**
Checks
Flight
Launch
Rocket
Safety

**7 LETTERS**
Engines

**8 LETTERS**
Controls
Thruster

**9 LETTERS**
Autopilot
Spacesuit

**12 LETTERS**
Acceleration

Place each of the words, from your preparation checklist on the opposite page, into the empty squares to create a filled crossword grid. Each word is used once so cross it off the list as you place it to help you keep track.

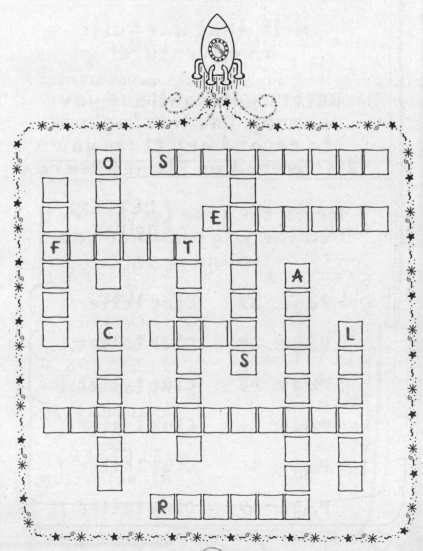

# CLUE LOGBOOK: PLANET PEDRA 202

### Well, that was quite an adventure!

Before you continue your journey, use this logbook to record any clues you discovered on Planet Pedra.

Write the clue letter next to the page number you found it on:

Page: 37    Clue letter: ◯

Page: 39    Clue letter: ◯

Page: 43    Clue letter: ◯

Page: 44    Clue letter: ◯

Page: 46    Clue letter: ◯

Page: 49    Clue letter: ◯

# NOTES

On your journey through the cosmos, you fly by all kinds of weird and wonderful planets.

Just look at this one! You don't know this planet's name (yet...)

It looks very futuristic and mysterious.

You weren't planning to land here, but who knows what will happen...?

Clue Logbook for this chapter is on page 78!

Oh no! One of your spacecraft's booster engines has broken!

Complete the number problems below and write your answers in the boxes. Each booster engine should have the same answer.
The odd one out needs fixing, but which one is it?

A. $12 \times 8 = \square$

B. $80 + 16 = \square$

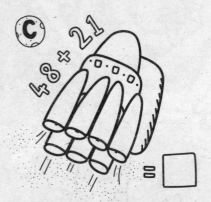

C. $48 + 21 = \square$

D. $32 \times 3 = \square$

To fix your broken booster engine, you need to make an emergency landing and search this mystery planet for spare parts.

Unscramble the letters in the words below to find out the names of the spare parts you need to collect. The first letters have been done for you and there are picture clues to help.

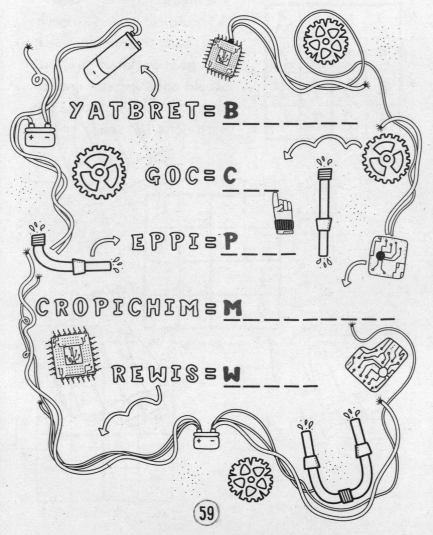

YATBRET = **B** _ _ _ _ _ _

GOC = **C** _ _ _

EPPI = **P** _ _ _ _

CROPICHIM = **M** _ _ _ _ _ _ _ _

REWIS = **W** _ _ _ _

You're welcomed to this new planet by a futuristic computer who calls itself 'The Mainframe'. You're excited to enter the big gates and explore but the Mainframe says it can't let you in until you've solved some puzzles...

In the sudoku grids below the numbers 1, 2, 3 and 4 should be added to each row, each column and each 2x2 bold outlined box, but should only appear once in each one. The first one has been done for you.

| 2 | 4 | 1 | 3 |
| 3 | 1 | 4 | 2 |
| 4 | 3 | 2 | 1 |
| 1 | 2 | 3 | 4 |

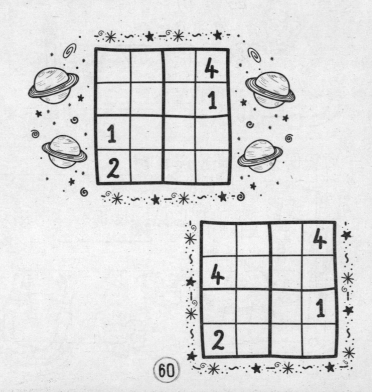

Wow, this planet looks so cool and futuristic! You wonder what the planet is called... The Mainframe gives you the name of the planet, but it's in code.

Crack the code below to reveal the name of this planet. (Then, if you like, you can also go back and add the planet's name to your map at the beginning of this book!)

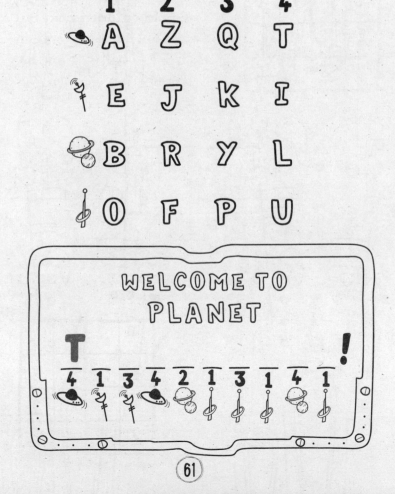

As you go through the gates, the first things you see are the Tek Towers.

Can you spot the six differences between the two pictures of the Tek Towers below?

Find your way through the maze from the top
of one tower to the bottom of the next tower.

START

FINISH

To collect the batteries you need, you must explore the underground tunnels of the Electric Cavern, where electricity is in the air (because batteries hang from the ceilings!).

Use one straight line to connect each kind of battery. You must visit each battery only once along the way. Whatever you do, don't travel along the same tunnel twice.

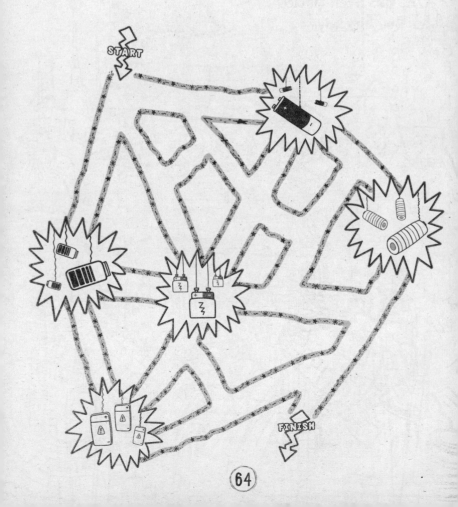

You'll find all the cogs you need on this Intergalactic Scrapheap. Earth isn't the only wasteful planet, they throw away useful things here too! Help the environment by reusing and recycling parts you need instead of buying new ones.

Circle all the cogs that are hidden in the picture of the Intergalactic Scrapheap below. One has been circled for you already.

You spend some time exploring the Intergalactic Scrapheap, looking at all the bizarre objects this alien planet has discarded.

Can you find the seven things below in the wordsearch on the opposite page? Words may be hidden horizontally or vertically.

BEAM BOLTS

LASER CUTTER

MOON GARAGE

ROCKET BOTTLES

SHIP CRUSHER

SPACE MAGNET

STAR CRANE

```
G R P T E T V O A I L U W
L O S H I P C R U S H E R
A C L B S W N S I Q E C L
S K R A K I I T Y S N V W
E E N J Z U J A U E S N B
R T L T S N S R F U U I E
C B N B O P S C S F D Q A
U O Y M F I S R O T J I M
T T M O O N G A R A G E B
T T Q A M W Y N U O U N O
E L P P P C E E R A L T L
R E S P A C E M A G N E T
T S O P O A G O U W H C S
```

Now you've collected the batteries and cogs
you need to fix your spacecraft, what's next?
Peculiar pipes!

Can you find your way from 'Start' to the centre of
the pipe maze then back out to 'Finish'?

Next you need to search for a microchip...

**Which pipe will take you all the way to Microworld? Write your answer in the box.**

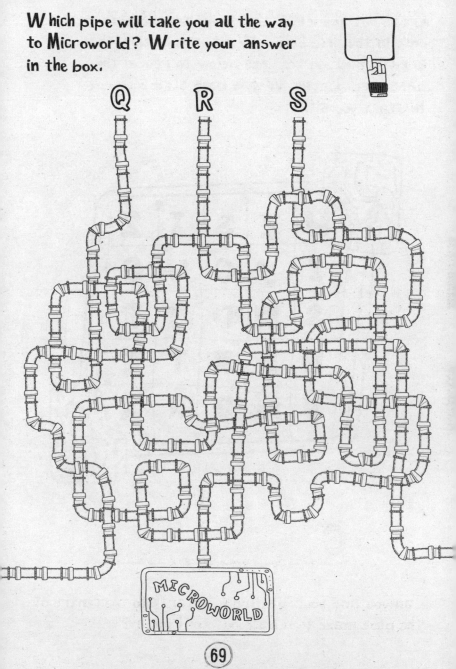

To enter Microworld, you need the password.

Cross out any letter that appears more than once in the grid below. Write the letters that are left over on the lines below to reveal the password. Letter W has been scribbled out to start you off.

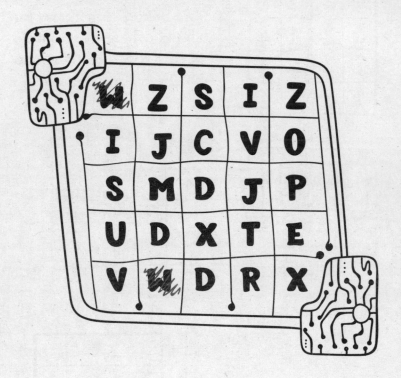

| W̶ | Z | S | I | Z |
|---|---|---|---|---|
| I | J | C | V | O |
| S | M | D | J | P |
| U | D | X | T | E |
| V | W̶ | D | R | X |

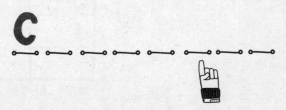

C _ _ _ _ _ _ _ _ _ _ _

Solve the sudokus below to collect the microchip you need for your spacecraft.

In the sudoku grids below, the numbers 1, 2, 3 and 4 should be added to each row, each column and each 2x2 bold outlined box, but should only appear once in each one. The first one has been done for you.

| 4 | 1 | 2 | 3 |
| 3 | 2 | 1 | 4 |
| 2 | 3 | 4 | 1 |
| 1 | 4 | 3 | 2 |

|  |  |  |  |
|  |  | 1 | 3 |
| 3 | 4 |  |  |
|  |  |  |  |

| 2 |  |  |  |
| 3 |  |  | 1 |
| 1 |  |  | 3 |
|  |  |  | 2 |

Welcome to the Tech Greenhouse! This is where robotic plants, digital flowers and other living alien machines grow. Isn't that awesome?

Follow the numbers up the stem of each tech plant and figure out which number is next in the sequence. Write the final number into the flower at the top of each stem.

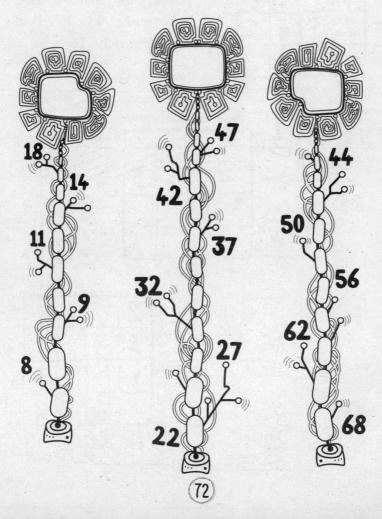

18
14
11
9
8

47
42
37
32
27
22

44
50
56
62
68

You have almost finished gathering all the parts you need to fix your spacecraft. The only thing left to collect is wire.

Can you find the wires hidden amongst the messy plantoids in the grid below? When you've found each one, write the grid reference next to it. One has been done for you.

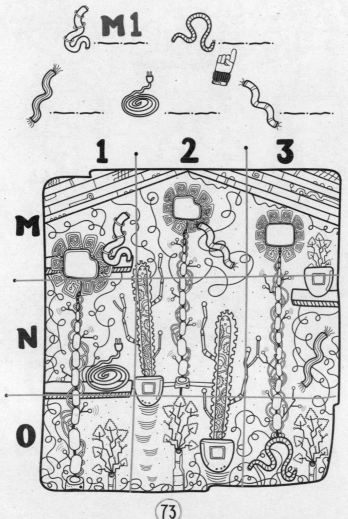

Now you have all the parts you need, let's hitch a ride on an asteroid bus to get back to your spacecraft.

**Which asteroid bus goes all the way to Bus Stop X16.782?**

Watch out! You need to dodge all of the other asteroids zooming past you on the way back...

You can move up, down or sideways, but you can't move diagonally and you must follow the asteroids in this order:

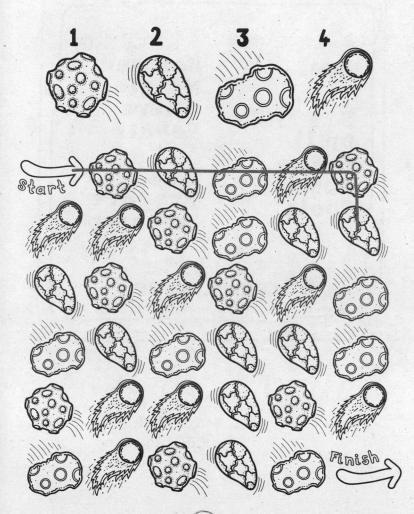

1    2    3    4

Start

Finish

Back at your spacecraft with all of the spare parts you collected on Tektropolo, it's time to do some repair work to prepare for the rest of your space journey!

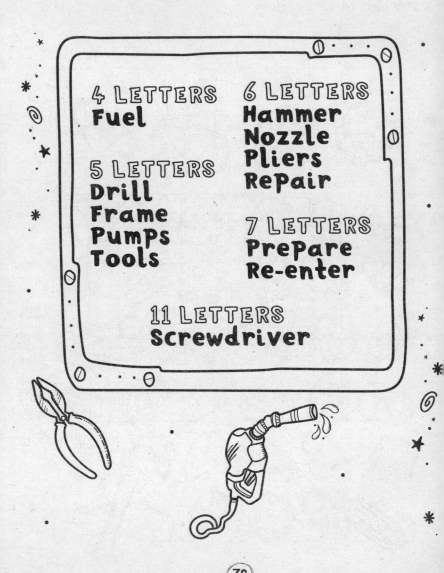

**4 LETTERS**
Fuel

**5 LETTERS**
Drill
Frame
Pumps
Tools

**6 LETTERS**
Hammer
Nozzle
Pliers
Repair

**7 LETTERS**
Prepare
Re-enter

**11 LETTERS**
Screwdriver

Place each of the words, from the checklist on the opposite page, into the empty squares to create a filled crossword grid. Each word is used once so cross it off the list as you place it to help you keep track.

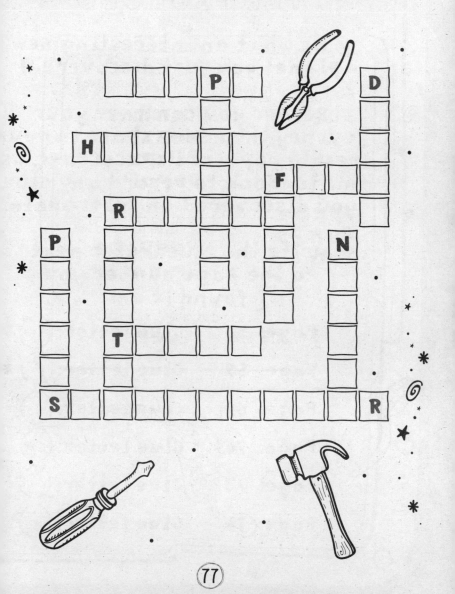

# *CLUE LOGBOOK:*
# TEKTROPOLO

Wow, what an interesting new planet you just discovered!

Before you continue your journey into deep space in your freshly repaired spacecraft, use this logbook to record any clues you discovered on Tektropolo.

Write the clue letter next to the page number you found it on:

Page: 58    Clue letter: ◯

Page: 59    Clue letter: ◯

Page: 69    Clue letter: ◯

Page: 70    Clue letter: ◯

Page: 73    Clue letter: ◯

Page: 74    Clue letter: ◯

# NOTES

You're now very deep into hyperspace, light years away from Earth!

Why not stop at the **INTERGALACTIC SPACE STATION** along the way?

It's time for some Space Station stumpers, microscope mind games and extraterrestrial experiments...

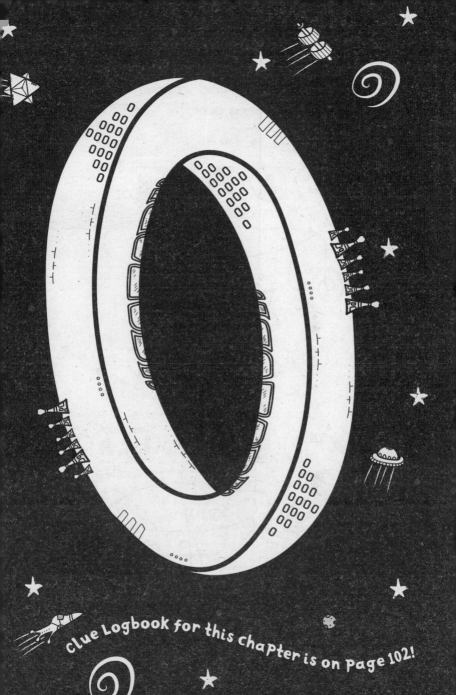

clue Logbook for this chapter is on Page 102!

Follow the lines and write the letter from each circle in the space at the end of each line to reveal some out-of-this-world words. Some letters have already been done for you.

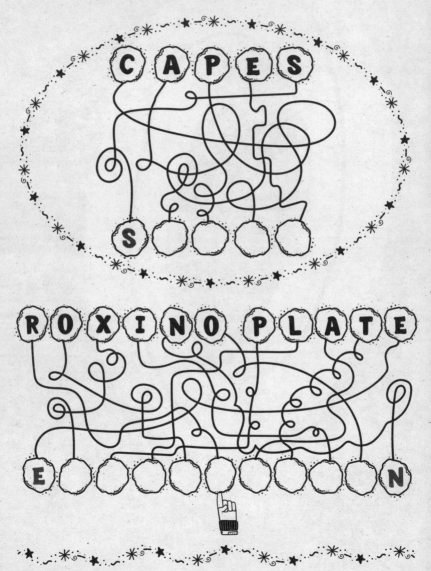

In the Dockyard of the Intergalactic Space Station, there are all kinds of starships, spacecraft and alien vehicles trying to find a place to park.

Can you match the spacecrafts to their correct docking spaces by looking at their shapes? One has been done for you.

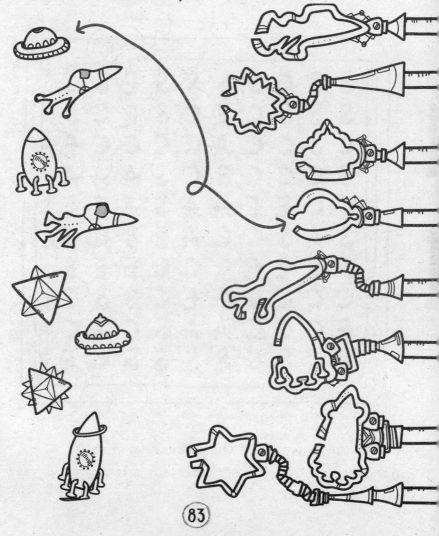

Now you've docked your spacecraft, you need to go through the Space Station's entrance.

To get in, find and circle the word:

# ACCESS

in the grid below.

S S C S S S S E S C
S S S C E C S E C S
C S C C A C C C C E
S C C C S C S A A A
C C E E A A S A C E
S A S C C A E S C C
A S E E C C C E E E
C C C C C E C S S C
E C C C A A S C S C
E C S C S S S S C E

Once you've accessed the entrance, you need to unlock the Space Station's four airlock doors...

To get the six-digit code to unlock each airlock
door, cross out any numbers that appear twice
in each grid below.

Then, write the left over numbers on the lines
below each grid, from top to bottom, and the
code will reveal itself! The first one has been
done for you.

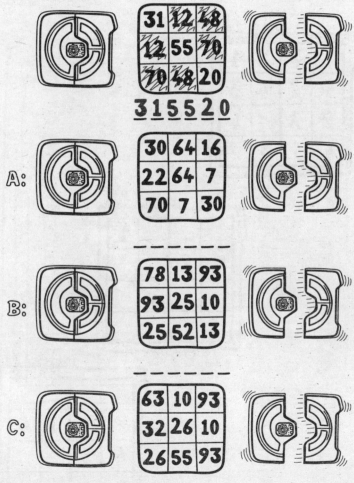

|     |     |     |
|-----|-----|-----|
| 31  | 12  | 48  |
| 12  | 55  | 70  |
| 70  | 48  | 20  |

<u>3 1 5 5 2 0</u>

A:

|     |     |     |
|-----|-----|-----|
| 30  | 64  | 16  |
| 22  | 64  | 7   |
| 70  | 7   | 30  |

– – – – – –

B:

|     |     |     |
|-----|-----|-----|
| 78  | 13  | 93  |
| 93  | 25  | 10  |
| 25  | 52  | 13  |

– – – – – –

C:

|     |     |     |
|-----|-----|-----|
| 63  | 10  | 93  |
| 32  | 26  | 10  |
| 26  | 55  | 93  |

– – – – – –

Once inside, you find yourself in the Control Centre, a place full of buttons, lights, levers, and of course, numbers!

In the sudoku grids below, the numbers 1, 2, 3 and 4 should be added to each row, each column and each 2x2 bold outlined box, but should only appear once in each one. The first one has been done for you.

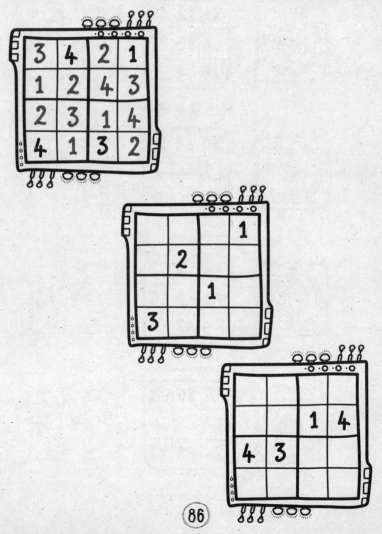

Press the buttons on the control panel to reveal a fact about the Intergalactic Space Station.

Look at the shapes of the buttons and use them as a key to find out which letters go where. Some letters have been done for you.

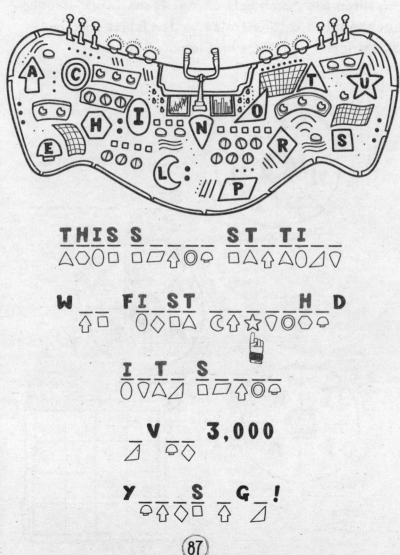

THIS S _ _ _ _     ST _ TI _ _

W _ _ FI _ ST _ _ _ _ _ _ H _ D

I _ T _ S _ _ _ _

_ V _ _ 3,000

Y _ _ _ S _ G _ !

100% of the Space Station's electricity is powered by renewable energy. (Energy from nature that won't run out and won't pollute planets or space.)

In the word-wheels, find the words for three things you can make renewable energy from...
Each word starts with the centre letter and uses all the letters in the wheel once.

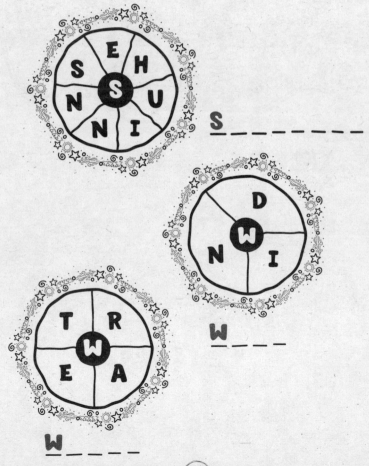

S _ _ _ _ _ _ _

W _ _ _ _

W _ _ _ _

In the Space Station's power room there are lots of different wind turbines for generating energy.

**W**hich silhouette correctly matches each turbine? Circle your answers.

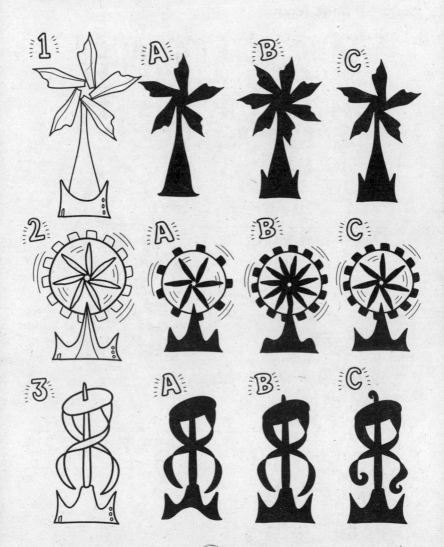

As you explore the Space Station, you meet two new kinds of aliens.

Use the key to crack the code and reveal the names of each alien species on this page. On the opposite page, use the same code to reveal the names of some strange foods.

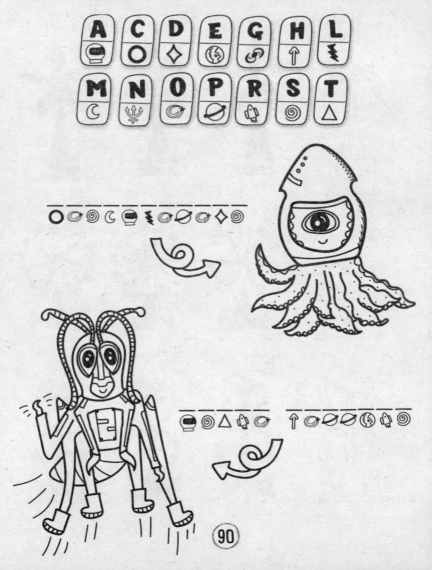

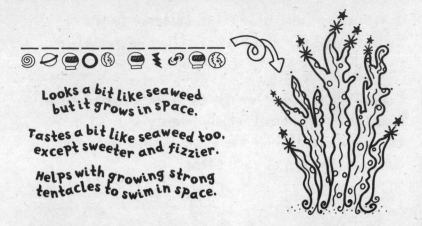

Looks a bit like seaweed but it grows in space.

Tastes a bit like seaweed too, except sweeter and fizzier.

Helps with growing strong tentacles to swim in space.

Like giant sweetcorn with a hint of stardust.

Eating it gives the ability to take massive leaps!

The aliens are very nice and friendly to you, because you're a new and interesting guest. However, you notice that the aliens seem angry with each other...

They tell you they've been arguing, because they are both trying to grow their food on board the Space Station, but the Space Garden is getting so overgrown that there isn't enough room for both food types!

You follow your new alien friends to the Space Garden, to see where they're growing their food.

Follow the numbers up through the stem of each plant and figure out which number is next in the sequence. Write the final number into the circle at the top of each stem.

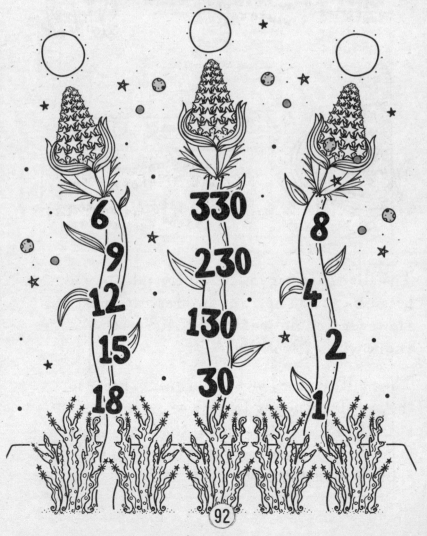

6
9
12
15
18

330
230
130
30

8
4
2
1

Maybe you can help the aliens by using science to create a new 'hybrid' food, joining both of their food types together so they can easily be grown in one garden.

Find your way through the maze from the Space Garden to the Lab to start your food experiments...

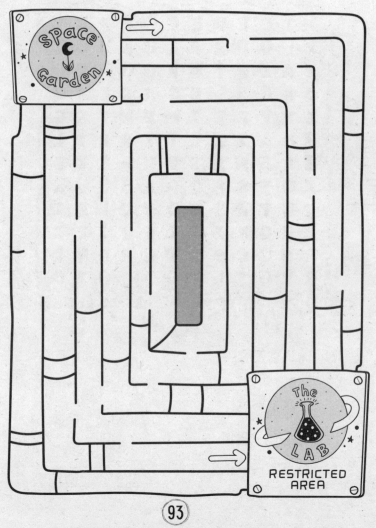

The Space Station Lab is full of equipment for your experiments.

In the wordsearch, can you find the eleven lab items from the list below?
Words may be hidden in the grid horizontally, vertically or diagonally.

```
M I C R O S C O P E B T
K L O P A P R O N U U G
R A E R T A R O O R T O
Q S C A L E S A R E E G
E X P E R I M E N T S G
Z H A I Y L T I A L T L
Z E A N A I P X A S T E
Z O J S A Q G A S O U S
J D T P T U Q T U L B I
A P G E F I E E Q I E I
R N G C D D P G R D O E
S T O T L T G O J O F C
```

APRON
EXPERIMENT
GAS
GOGGLES
INSPECT
JARS

LIQUID
MICROSCOPE
SCALES
SOLID
TEST TUBE

# You have more experimenting to do!

You can move up, down or sideways, but you can't move diagonally and you must follow the test tubes in this order:

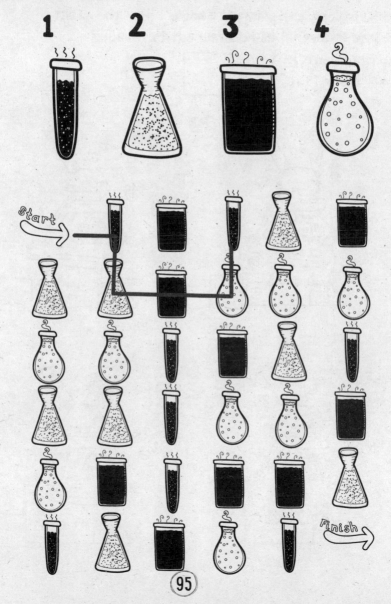

You've nearly finished creating a hybrid food!
All of your experiments are going well, except
one. Let's take a closer look...

Complete the number problems below. Each
microscope experiment should show the exact
same answer. The odd one out is a failed
experiment, but
which one is it?

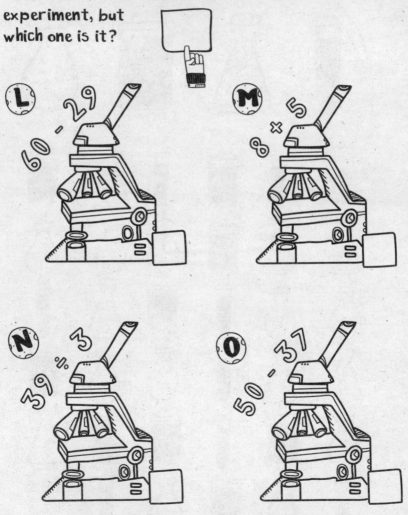

L 60 - 29

M 8 × 5

N 39 % 3

O 50 - 31

Under the microscope, you can see lots of strange things happening in your experiments!

Can you spot the six differences between these two pictures below?

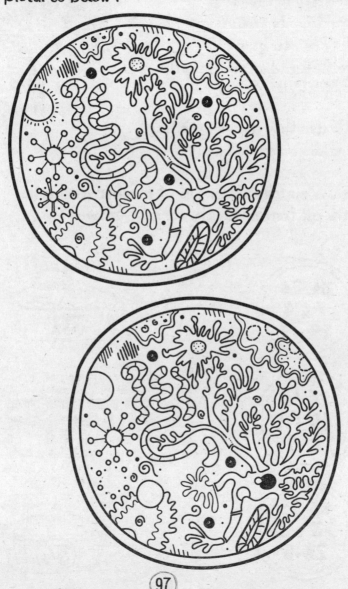

You did it!

In the Lab, you made a new food mixing Star Corn and Space Algae that the Cosmalopods and Astro Hoppers can grow together and share happily. Nice work!

Let's use this new ingredient to make some lovely pie!

Can you match each group of number problems to the pie containing the correct answer?

64-36
7 x 4
19 + 9

76-42
68 ÷ 2
19 + 15

56-25
93 ÷ 3
26+5

31

28

34

There are lots of hungry aliens waiting in the Space Station canteen. They want to try your new food!

Use one straight line to connect each of the canteen tables. You must visit each table only once along the way. Whatever you do, don't travel along the same path twice!

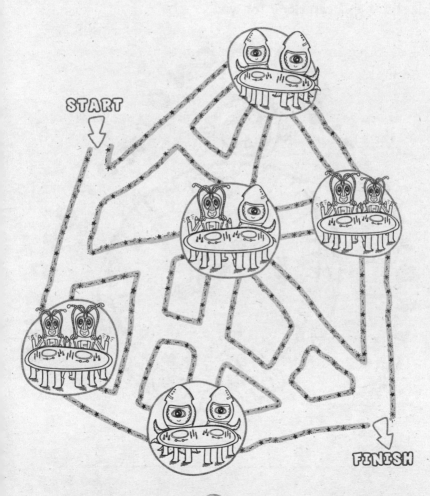

START

FINISH

Before you leave, the aliens aboard the Space Station want to give you a gift! This is to say thanks for your help, and also to guide you to your next destination...

Scribble out every other letter. Write the letters that are left over on the lines below to spell out the name of the gift. The first letter has been done for you.

C _ _ _ _ _ _   _ _ _ _ _ _ _

Instead of walking all the way back to the Dockyard to get into your spacecraft, you can just slide down one of the station's Space Flumes instead. What a fun shortcut!

**Which Space Flume slide leads back to your docked spacecraft?**

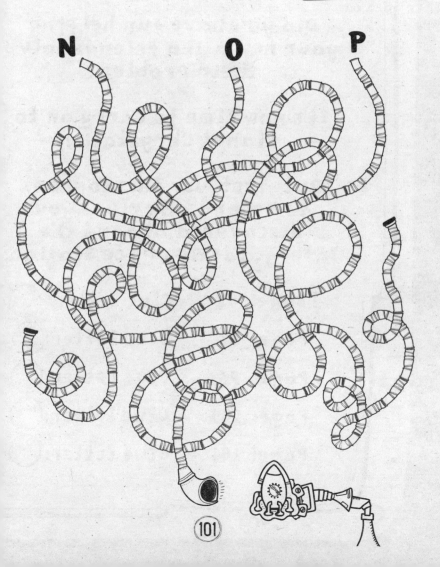

# ☆〰CLUE LOGBOOK:〰☆
# INTERGALACTIC
# SPACE STATION

Did you have fun helping
your new alien friends solve
their problem?

It's now time to carry on to
Planet Chrystalis!

But first, use this logbook
to record any clues you
discovered aboard the
Intergalactic Space Station:

Page: 82    Clue letter: ◯

Page: 87    Clue letter: ◯

Page: 96    Clue letter: ◯

Page: 100   Clue letter: ◯

Page: 101   Clue letter: ◯

**NOTES**

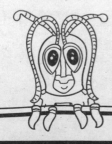

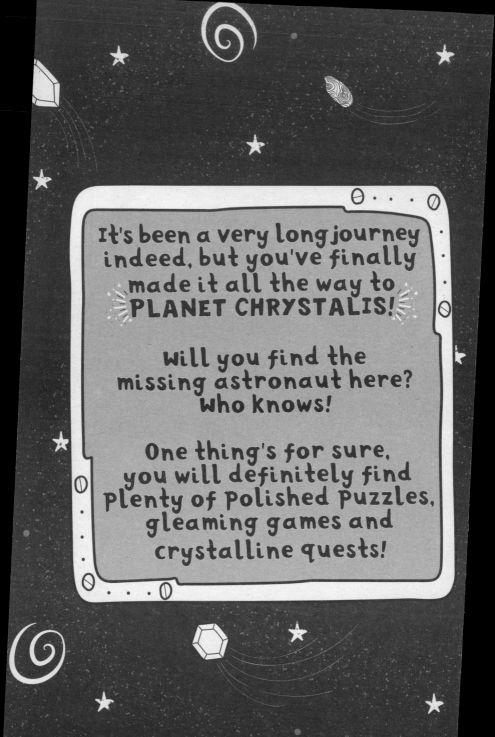

clue Logbook for this chapter is on Page 126!

Can you spot the six differences between these two pictures of your view on **Planet Chrystalis?**

As soon as you set foot on the planet you notice them: footprints! And they're not strange alien footprints this time, they're big space boot footprints... Could they belong to the missing astronaut?

Which of the tangled paths below leads to the footprints? Write your answer in the box.

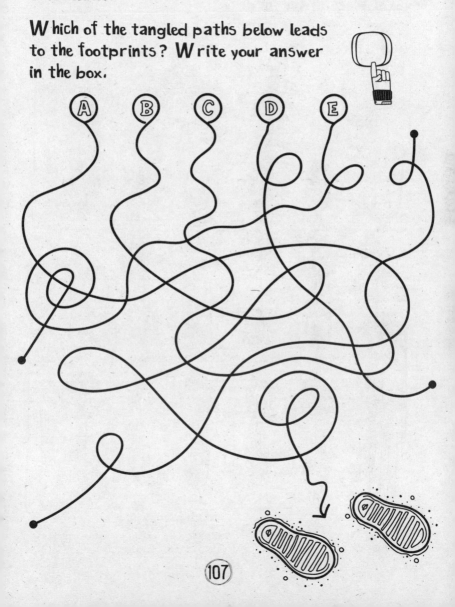

Follow the footprints through the impressive crystal forests of Planet Chrystalis...

You can move up, down or sideways, but you can't move diagonally and you must follow the crystal trees in this order:

**1**   **2**   **3**   **4**

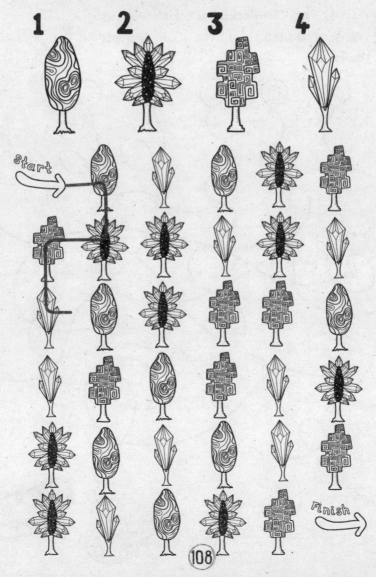

Can you make your way through the maze of roots below this crystal tree to get to the deep and mossy supercaves?

START

FINISH

Can you match each group of words to the cave containing the correct missing letter? The first one has been done for you.

ROOTS
HOLLOW
MOSS

_LIMB
RO_KY
_AVERN

_CHO
D_EP
_MPTY

B_TS
S_NDY
C_NYON

_TONE
FO_SIL
_PIDER

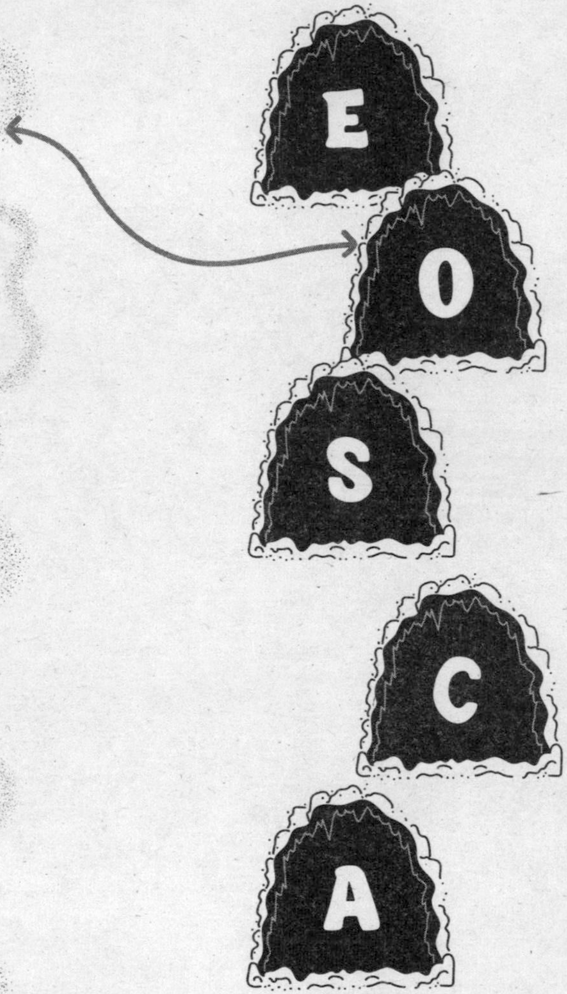

E

O

S

C

A

Now, match each group of number problems to the cave containing the correct answer. Again, the first one has been done for you.

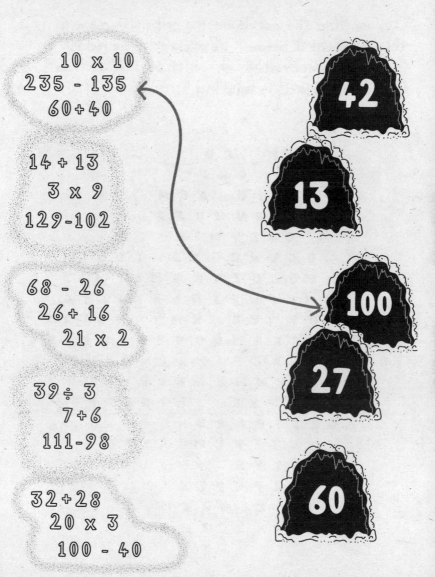

10 x 10
235 - 135
60 + 40

14 + 13
3 x 9
129 - 102

68 - 26
26 + 16
21 x 2

39 ÷ 3
7 + 6
111 - 98

32 + 28
20 x 3
100 - 40

42

13

100

27

60

You follow the footprints out of the supercaves to the edge of Diamond Dust Ridge. Be brave, it's time to parachute jump!

Can you find the words on the opposite page in the wordsearch below? Words may be hidden in the grid horizontally or vertically. Watch out! One of the words is missing.

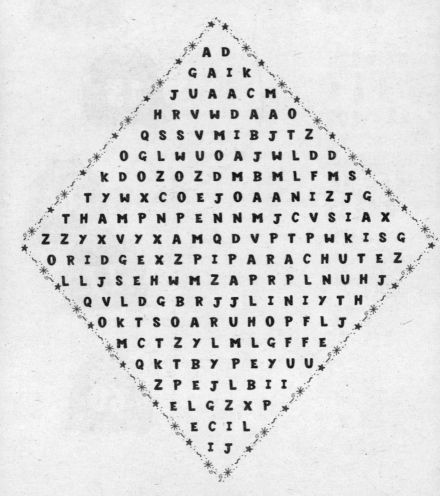

```
            A D
           G A I K
          J U A A C M
         H R V W D A A O
        Q S S V M I B J T Z
       O G L W U O A J W L D D
      K D O Z O Z D M B M L F M S
     T Y W X C O E J O A A N I Z J G
    T H A M P N P E N N M J C V S I A X
   Z Z Y X V Y X A M Q D V P T P W K I S G
  O R I D G E X Z P I P A R A C H U T E Z
   L L J S E H W M Z A P R P L N U H J
    Q V L D G B R J J L I N I Y T H
     O K T S O A R U H O P F L J
      M C T Z Y L M L G F F E
       Q K T B Y P E Y U U
        Z P E J L B I I
         E L G Z X P
          E C I L
           I J
```

DIAMOND

RIDGE

JUMP

PARACHUTE

SOAR

SWOOP

CLIFF

DROP

**W**rite the missing word here.

_ _ _ _ _

Oops! As you fly down into the valley, your parachute gets caught in all the vines.

Follow the tangled vines. Which one leads you out of this mess?

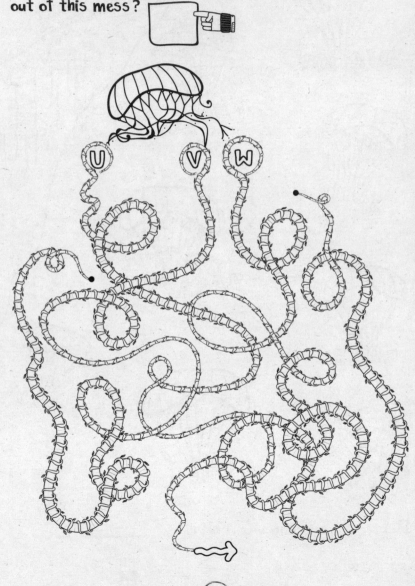

Not so fast. If you truly want to leave the
Valley of Vines, you'll have to find your way
through this viney maze from start to finish...

START

FINISH

When you finally escape the Valley of Vines, you find yourself standing in front of the tall and spikey Thorny Mountains.

Follow the numbers up each mountain and figure out which number is next in the sequence. Write the final number into the triangle at the top of each mountain.

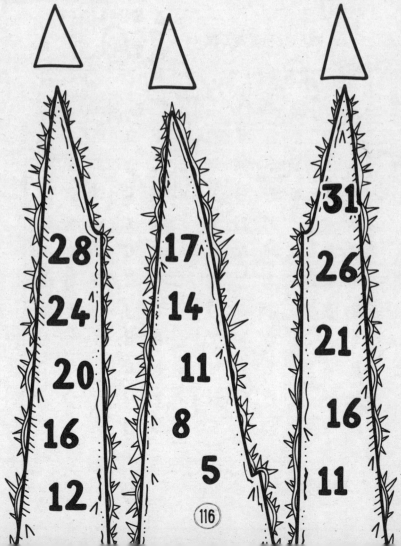

28
24
20
16
12

17
14
11
8
5

31
26
21
16
11

Can you find all nine words below in the Thorny Mountain wordsearch? Words may be hidden in the grid horizontally or vertically.

△ CANYON

△ CLIMB

△ HIKE

△ MOUNTAIN

△ PEAK

△ POINTY

△ SPIKED

△ SUMMIT

△ THORN

| T | O | J | L | I | H | S | P | I | K | E | D |
|---|---|---|---|---|---|---|---|---|---|---|---|
| A | P | T | S | M | I | L | C | J | B | I | S |
| Y | I | X | U | O | K | K | U | Q | D | A | F |
| J | R | P | M | U | E | H | R | E | R | N | V |
| R | K | L | M | N | K | G | E | G | J | S | R |
| X | L | C | I | T | W | C | L | I | M | B | W |
| S | E | L | T | A | O | G | C | J | P | L | N |
| L | I | A | O | I | T | V | A | S | O | K | V |
| A | E | F | P | N | S | N | N | C | I | S | D |
| K | T | H | O | R | N | U | Y | G | N | C | S |
| H | N | T | L | T | E | D | O | H | T | L | Y |
| T | P | E | A | K | S | A | N | B | Y | F | M |

On the other side of the Thorny Mountains, you follow the footprints all the way to the edge of a gleaming Emerald Lagoon. The sunlight is reflecting off the water and crystals. It's beautiful!

In the word-wheels, find three other words you could use to describe the shimmering lagoon. Each word starts with the centre letter and uses all the letters in the wheel once.

S _ _ _ _ _

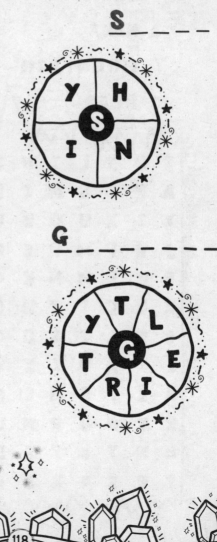

G _ _ _ _ _ _ _

S _ _ _ _ _ _

Follow the lines and write the letter from each circle in the space at the end of each line to reveal the names of two crystals. Some letters have already been done for you.

# Which of these alien boats will take you across Emerald Lagoon to the X-shaped Island?

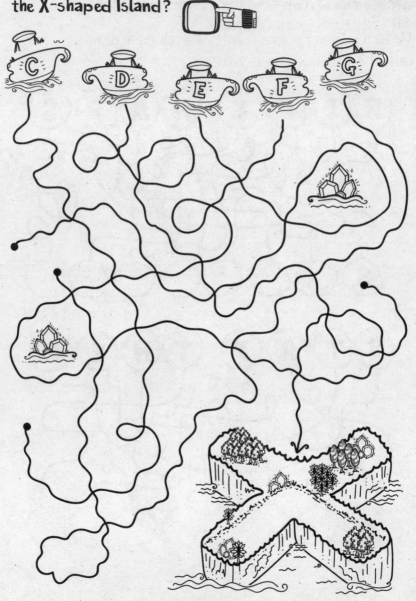

On your boat journey across the gleaming lagoon you notice all sorts of alien objects under the water.

**W**hich silhouettes correctly match each sunken object? Circle your answers.

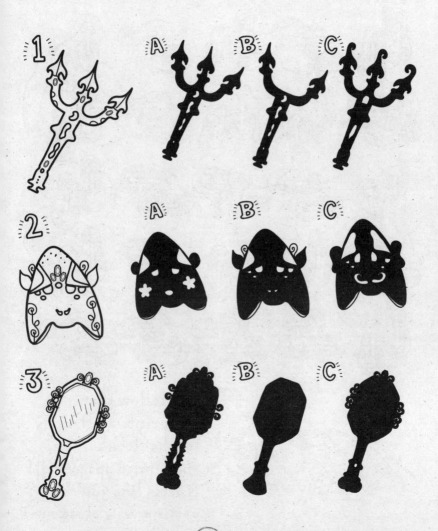

On the X-shaped island, you find LOTS more footprints!

Can you find a path to follow the footprints from start to finish, only going in the direction of the arrows?

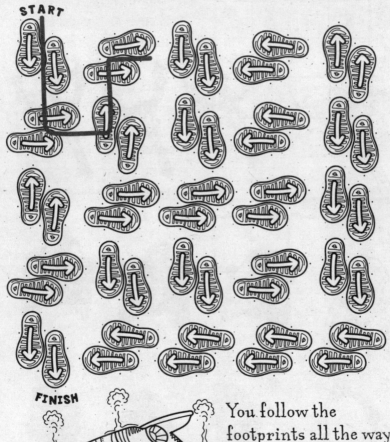

START

FINISH

You follow the footprints all the way to what looks like an abandoned spacecraft! It feels like you're getting very close now...

You can't get into the abandoned spacecraft to explore it unless you unlock the emergency hatch. Find the door code by solving the puzzle below.

In the sudoku grids, the numbers 1, 2, 3 and 4 should be added to each row, each column and each 2x2 bold outlined box, but should only appear once in each one. The first one has been done for you.

| 1 | 4 | 3 | 2 |
| 3 | 2 | 1 | 4 |
| 4 | 3 | 2 | 1 |
| 2 | 1 | 4 | 3 |

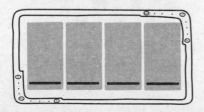

Write down the numbers from the shaded squares from left to right to reveal the door code.

Use the symbol key below to crack the code and fill in the missing letters below...

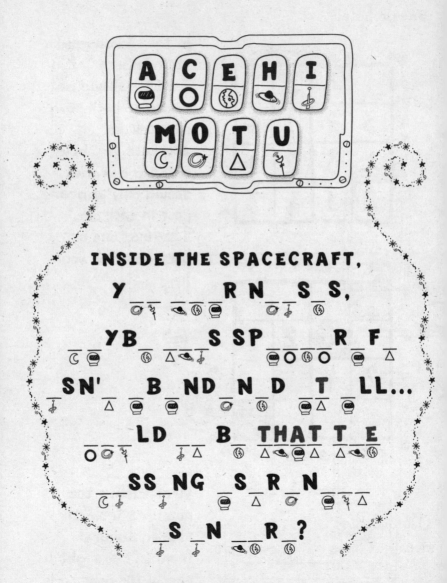

The inside of the spacecraft is so much bigger than it seemed from the outside, look at how many doors there are.

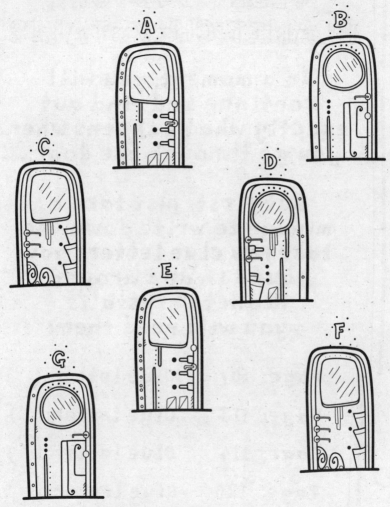

Odd one out: which of the doors above does not have a matching pair?

The answer is the door you go through next...

# ☆⌁CLUE LOGBOOK:⌁☆
# PLANET CHRYSTALIS

In a moment, you will continue and find out exactly what happens when you go through the door...

But first, just take a minute to write down the last few clue letters you found in and around Planet Chrystalis – you will need them!

Page: 107    Clue letter: ◯

Page: 113    Clue letter: ◯

Page: 114    Clue letter: ◯

Page: 120    Clue letter: ◯

## The story continues...

As you go through the strange door inside the spacecraft, you meet someone wearing a spacesuit!

You've certainly found an astronaut! But is it the astronaut you have been looking for?

Crack the code on the next pages to reveal the end of the story...

# Crack the code to finish the story!

**Look back at all five Clue Logbooks on Pages 30, 54, 78, 102 and 126. Write the clue letters into the key below:**

(For example, because you found the letter 'V' on Page 12, the letter 'V' is in the '12' box)

Once your key is complete, you can crack the code to reveal the story ending!

# THEY TAKE OFF THEIR SPACE HELMET...

YOU _____ THE
$\overline{120}\ \overline{73}\ \overline{87}\ \overline{74}\ \overline{113}$

$\overline{100}\ \overline{27}\ \overline{69}\ \overline{69}\ \overline{27}\ \overline{74}\ \overline{59}$ $\overline{49}\ \overline{69}\ \overline{70}\ \overline{82}\ \overline{73}\ \overline{74}\ \overline{49}\ \overline{87}\ \overline{70}$

BUT THEIR _____ STARTS TO CHANGE...
$\overline{120}\ \overline{49}\ \overline{58}\ \overline{44}$

WHAT A $\overline{69}\ \overline{70}\ \overline{82}\ \overline{49}\ \overline{74}\ \overline{59}\ \overline{44}$ $\overline{58}\ \overline{73}\ \overline{96}\ \overline{73}\ \overline{87}\ \overline{82}$ ...

SO MANY _____!
$\overline{44}\ \overline{22}\ \overline{44}\ \overline{69}$

## HOW CAN THIS BE? YOU REALISE THAT THEY WERE AN

IN

$\overline{49}\ \overline{96}\ \overline{27}\ \overline{44}\ \overline{74}$ $\overline{113}\ \overline{27}\ \overline{69}\ \overline{59}\ \overline{87}\ \overline{27}\ \overline{69}\ \overline{44}$

## ALL ALONG!

$\overline{101}\ \overline{96}\ \overline{49}\ \overline{74}\ \overline{44}\ \overline{70}$ $\overline{58}\ \overline{21}\ \overline{82}\ \overline{22}\ \overline{69}\ \overline{70}\ \overline{49}\ \overline{96}\ \overline{27}\ \overline{69}$

IS THEIR TRUE _____.
$\overline{21}\ \overline{73}\ \overline{100}\ \overline{44}$

YOU _____ YOUR
$\overline{58}\ \overline{73}\ \overline{100}\ \overline{101}\ \overline{96}\ \overline{44}\ \overline{70}\ \overline{44}\ \overline{113}$

_____, BUT NOW, CAN YOU
$\overline{100}\ \overline{27}\ \overline{69}\ \overline{69}\ \overline{27}\ \overline{73}\ \overline{74}$

KEEP THEIR _____?
$\overline{69}\ \overline{44}\ \overline{58}\ \overline{82}\ \overline{44}\ \overline{70}$

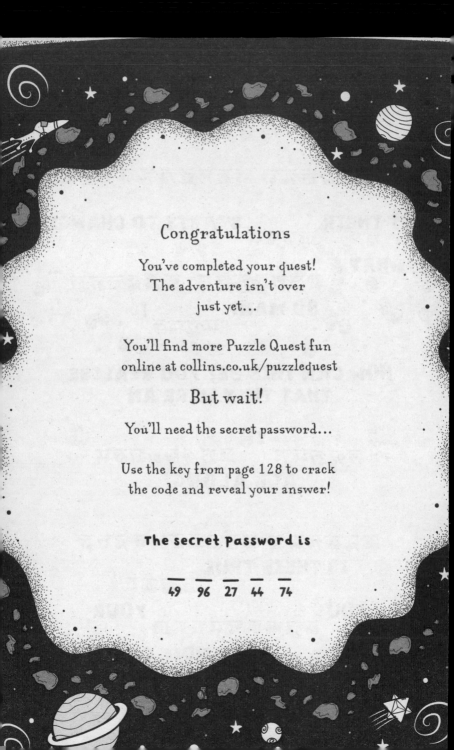

# Congratulations

You've completed your quest!
The adventure isn't over
just yet...

You'll find more Puzzle Quest fun
online at collins.co.uk/puzzlequest

## But wait!

You'll need the secret password...

Use the key from page 128 to crack
the code and reveal your answer!

**The secret password is**

$\overline{49}$ $\overline{96}$ $\overline{27}$ $\overline{44}$ $\overline{74}$

# Puzzle
## Answers

# Page 10 – Word Tangle

## MISSING

## ASTRONAUT

# Page 12 – Wordfinder Puzzle

## GRAVITY

### Page 13 – Maths Game

clockwise

anticlockwise

clockwise

### Page 11 – Maze

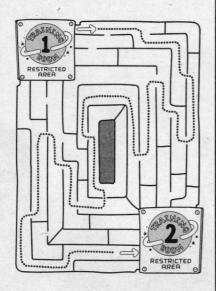

## Page 14 – Word Scramble

O N M
O N
‾ ‾ ‾ ‾
**MOON**

T S L
N P A E
‾ ‾ ‾ ‾ ‾ ‾ ‾
**PLANETS**

T A
R S
‾ ‾ ‾ ‾
**STAR**

U R J E I P T
‾ ‾ ‾ ‾ ‾ ‾ ‾
**JUPITER**

R A M
S
‾ ‾ ‾ ‾
**MARS**

S E A T I D O
R
‾ ‾ ‾ ‾ ‾ ‾ ‾ ‾
**ASTEROID**

## Page 16 – Spot the Difference

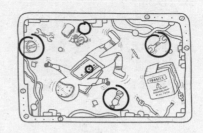

## Page 15 – Wordsearch

```
B A C K F L I P k x
S O M E R S A U L T
A x R N x G L I D E
E A O Y S U N F D S
L U L x B D D L I P
D D L E A P R O H I
F B O U N C E A Q N
L R V T W I S T S I
Y K E R F L M A T A
S S R A H E C T R U
```

## Page 17 – Silhouette Match

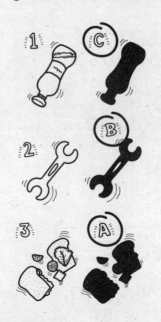

(133)

## Page 18 – Word-Wheels

**BURGER**

**ICE CREAM**

**PIZZA**

## Page 19 – Word Scramble

MOON
MUSHROOM SOUP

TELESCOPE
TOMATO SOUP

SUN
SPAGHETTI

MARS
MACARONI

COMET
COOKIES

ASTRONAUT
APPLE PIE

## Pages 20 & 21 – Kriss Kross

```
        B A C K P A C K     G
      M           A         L
      I     S P E A K E R   O
W     C     P               V
A I R T A N K       S       E
T     O     C       T U B E S
E     P     E       U
R     H   S U N V I S O R
T     O     U       H       B
A     N     I     R A D I O O
N     E     T       D       O
K                   E       T
      E A R P H O N E S     S
```

## Page 22 – Find It

 **Y3**

 **Y1**

 **Z2**

 **X1**

 **Y2**

Page 23 – Sock Game

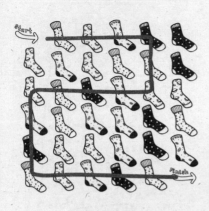

Page 24 – Code Puzzle

# TIME TO TAKE THE SPACE BUGGY FOR A TEST DRIVE

Page 25 – Maze

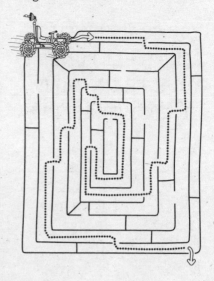

Page 26 – Sudoku

| 2 | 1 | 4 | 3 |
| 4 | 3 | 1 | 2 |
| 3 | 4 | 2 | 1 |
| 1 | 2 | 3 | 4 |

| 1 | 3 | 4 | 2 |
| 2 | 4 | 3 | 1 |
| 4 | 1 | 2 | 3 |
| 3 | 2 | 1 | 4 |

| 4 | 3 | 1 | 2 |
| 1 | 2 | 3 | 4 |
| 2 | 1 | 4 | 3 |
| 3 | 4 | 2 | 1 |

## Page 27 – Code-Cracker

YOU CRACKED THE
CODE WELL DONE!
YOUR TRAINING IS
ALMOST COMPLETE.

A – 8
C – 12
D – 19
E – 15
H – 17
I – 13
K – 5

L – 6
N – 1
O – 2
R – 10
T – 3
U – 7

## Page 28 – Launch Sequence

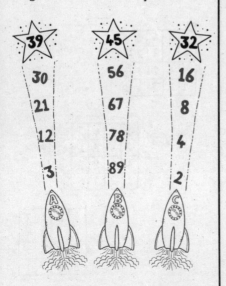

## Page 29 – Wordsearch

## Page 34 – Maze

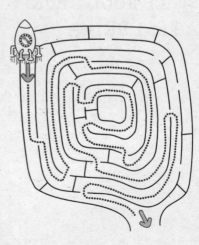

136

## Page 35 – Silhouette Match

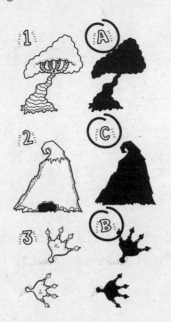

## Page 36 – Spot the Difference

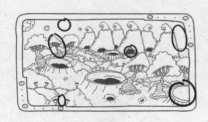

## Page 37 – Tangled Paths

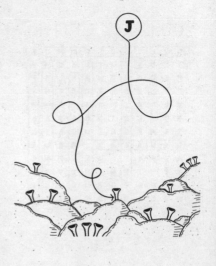

## Page 38 – Hot Spring Sequence

## Page 39 – Word Scribble

# DON'T LOOK DOWN!

## Pages 40 & 41 – Wordsearch

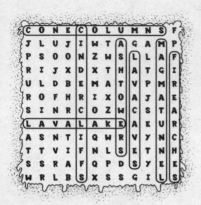

## Page 43 – Maths Game

Spikey field Q has the lowest danger total

## Page 42 – Sudoku

| 3 | 4 | 1 | 2 |
|---|---|---|---|
| 1 | 2 | 3 | 4 |
| 4 | 3 | 2 | 1 |
| 2 | 1 | 4 | 3 |

| 1 | 2 | 3 | 4 |
|---|---|---|---|
| 3 | 4 | 1 | 2 |
| 2 | 3 | 4 | 1 |
| 4 | 1 | 2 | 3 |

| 4 | 1 | 2 | 3 |
|---|---|---|---|
| 3 | 2 | 4 | 1 |
| 2 | 3 | 1 | 4 |
| 1 | 4 | 3 | 2 |

## Page 44 – Odd One Out

## Page 45 – Code-Cracker

"WE'LL ONLY HELP YOU IF:
YOU USE YOUR SPACECRAFT TO COLLECT SOME MOONBLOOM SEEDS FOR US!"

## Page 47 – Word Tangle

CRATER

CRESCENT MOON

## Page 46 – Maths Game

V 56

W 57

X 55

Y 54

## Page 48 – Moonbloom Game

## Page 49 – Wordfinder Puzzle

### DANGER

## Page 51 – Word Tangle

Yes, you were (C)(H)(A)(S)(E)(D)

by a bear from (S)(P)(A)(C)(E)

with moons on its (H)(E)(A)(D).

You gave it some (B)(R)(E)(A)(D).

With something to (E)(A)(T),

it left you in (P)(E)(A)(C)(E).

Not even a (S)(C)(R)(A)(P)(E),

What a lucky (E)(S)(C)(A)(P)(E)!

## Page 50 – Moonbear Maze

## Pages 52 & 53 – Kriss Kross

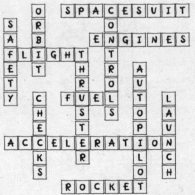

## Page 58 – Engine Maths

(A) ≅ **96**   (B) ≅ **96**

(C) ≅ **69**   (D) ≅ **96**

Engine C needs fixing

## Page 59 – Word Scramble

YATBRET ≅ **BATTERY**

GOC ≅ **COG**

EPPI ≅ **PIPE**

CROPICHIM ≅ **MICROCHIP**

REWIS ≅ **WIRES**

## Page 60 – Sudoku

| 2 | 4 | 1 | 3 |
|---|---|---|---|
| 3 | 1 | 4 | 2 |
| 4 | 3 | 2 | 1 |
| 1 | 2 | 3 | 4 |

| 3 | 1 | 2 | 4 |
|---|---|---|---|
| 4 | 2 | 3 | 1 |
| 1 | 3 | 4 | 2 |
| 2 | 4 | 1 | 3 |

| 1 | 2 | 3 | 4 |
|---|---|---|---|
| 4 | 3 | 1 | 2 |
| 3 | 4 | 2 | 1 |
| 2 | 1 | 4 | 3 |

## Page 61 – Code-Cracker

WELCOME TO PLANET TEKTROPOLO!

## Page 62 – Spot the Difference

## Page 63 – Maze

## Page 64 – Maze

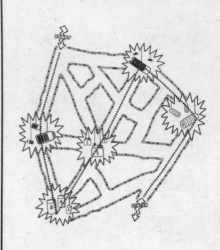

## Page 65 – Spot the Cog

## Pages 66 & 67 – Wordsearch

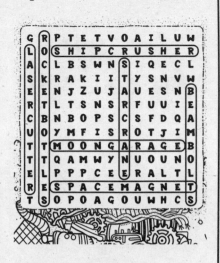

## Page 68 – Maze

## Page 69 – Tangled Pipes

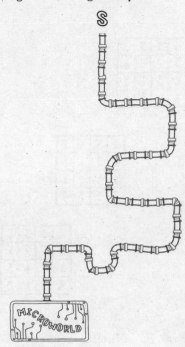

## Page 70 – Wordfinder Puzzle

# COMPUTER

## Page 71 – Sudoku

| 4 | 1 | 2 | 3 |
|---|---|---|---|
| 3 | 2 | 1 | 4 |
| 2 | 3 | 4 | 1 |
| 1 | 4 | 3 | 2 |

| 1 | 3 | 4 | 2 |
|---|---|---|---|
| 4 | 2 | 1 | 3 |
| 3 | 4 | 2 | 1 |
| 2 | 1 | 3 | 4 |

| 2 | 1 | 3 | 4 |
|---|---|---|---|
| 3 | 4 | 2 | 1 |
| 1 | 2 | 4 | 3 |
| 4 | 3 | 1 | 2 |

## Page 72 – Number Sequence

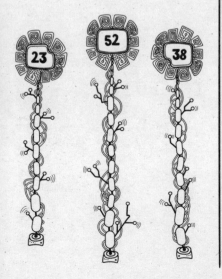

## Page 73 – Code Finder

## Page 74 – Tangled Bus Routes

## Page 75 – Asteroid Game

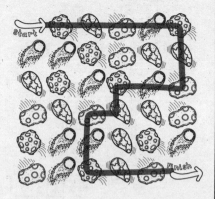

## Pages 76 & 77 – Kriss Kross

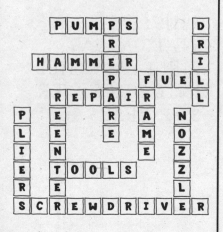

## Page 82 – Word Tangle

SPACE

EXPLORATION

## Page 83 – Shape Match

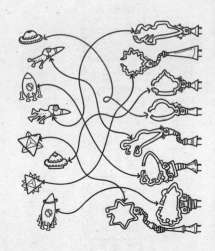

## Page 84 – Wordfinder

## Page 85 – Maths Game

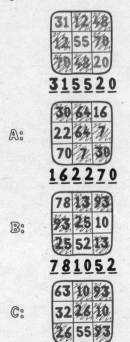

**315520**

A: **162270**

B: **781052**

C: **633255**

## Page 86 – Sudoku

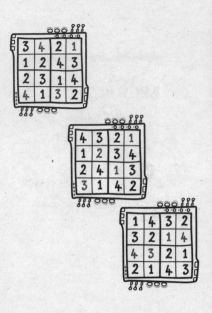

## Page 87 – Code-Cracker

# THIS SPACE STATION WAS FIRST LAUNCHED INTO SPACE OVER 3,000 YEARS AGO!

**SUNSHINE**

**WATER**

**WIND**

# COSMALOPODS
# ASTRO HOPPERS

# SPACE ALGAE
# STAR CORN

## Page 92 – Plant Sequence

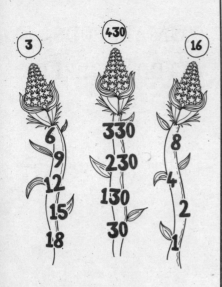

## Page 93 – Maze

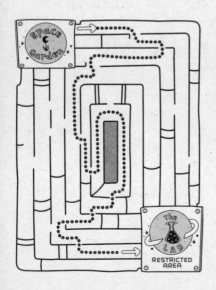

## Page 94 – Wordsearch

## Page 95 – Test Tube Game

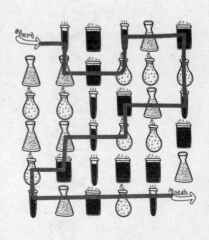

## Page 96 – Microscope Maths

**L** = **31**  **M** = **13**

**N** = **13**  **O** = **13**

The failed experiment is L

## Page 98 – Maths Game

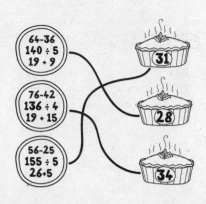

## Page 97 – Spot the Difference

## Page 99 – Maze

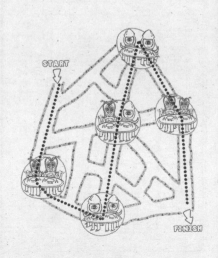

Page 100 – Word Scribble

# CRYSTAL COMPASS

Page 106 – Spot the Difference

Page 101 –Tangled Paths

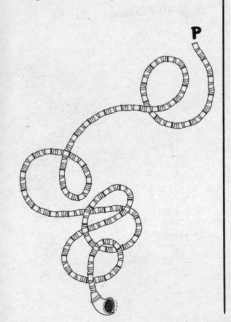

Page 107 – Tangled Paths

## Page 108 – Crystal Tree Game

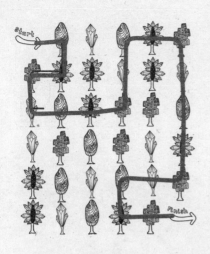

## Page 110 – Word Game

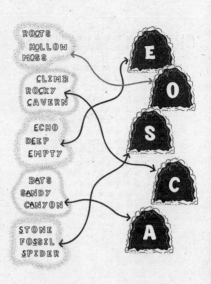

## Page 109 – Maze

## Page 111 – Maths Game

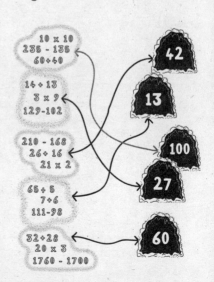

## Pages 112 & 113– Wordsearch

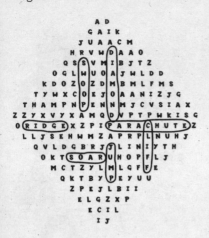

## Page 114 – Tangled Vines

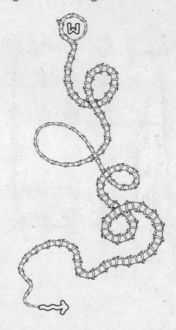

## Page 113 – Missing Word

DROP

## Page 115 – Maze

## Page 116 – Mountain Sequence

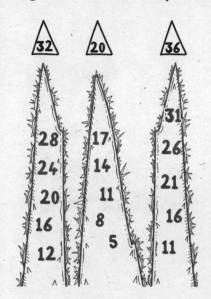

## Page 117 – Wordsearch

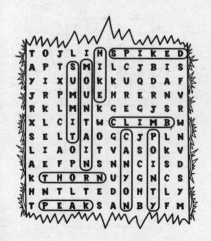

## Page 118 – Word-Wheels

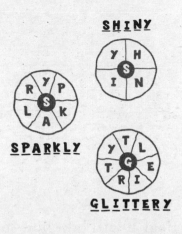

**SHINY**

**SPARKLY**

**GLITTERY**

## Page 119 – Word Tangle

SAPPHIRE

AMETHYST

## Page 120 – Boat Tangle

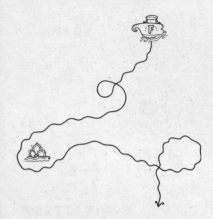

Boat F will take you to the island

## Page 121 – Silhoutte Match

## Page 122 – Footprint Game

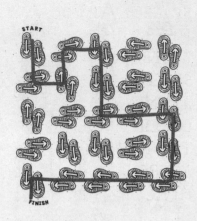

## Page 123 – Sudoku

| 1 | 4 | 3 | 2 |
|---|---|---|---|
| 3 | 2 | 1 | 4 |
| 4 | 3 | 2 | 1 |
| 2 | 1 | 4 | 3 |

| 1 | 2 | 3 | 4 |
|---|---|---|---|
| 4 | 3 | 2 | 1 |
| 2 | 4 | 1 | 3 |
| 3 | 1 | 4 | 2 |

| 1 | 3 | 1 | 2 |
|---|---|---|---|

INSIDE THE
SPACECRAFT, YOU
HEAR NOISES.
MAYBE THIS
SPACECRAFT ISN'T
ABANDONED AT ALL...
COULD IT BE THAT
THE MISSING
ASTRONAUT IS IN
HERE ?

THEY TAKE OFF
THEIR SPACE
HELMET...

YOU FOUND THE
MISSING ASTRONAUT!

BUT THEIR FACE
STARTS TO CHANGE...
WHAT A STRANGE
COLOUR...
SO MANY EYES!

HOW CAN THIS BE?
YOU REALISE THAT
THEY WERE AN
ALIEN IN DISGUISE
ALL ALONG!

PLANET CHRYSTALIS
IS THEIR TRUE HOME.

YOU COMPLETED
YOUR MISSION, BUT
NOW, CAN YOU KEEP
THEIR SECRET?

# NOTES

(Blank 'notes' pages like this are handy for jotting down any notes or working out when you're busy solving puzzles!

You could also use them to write, doodle, or for anything else you like while on your space quest!)

....*~MMMMM

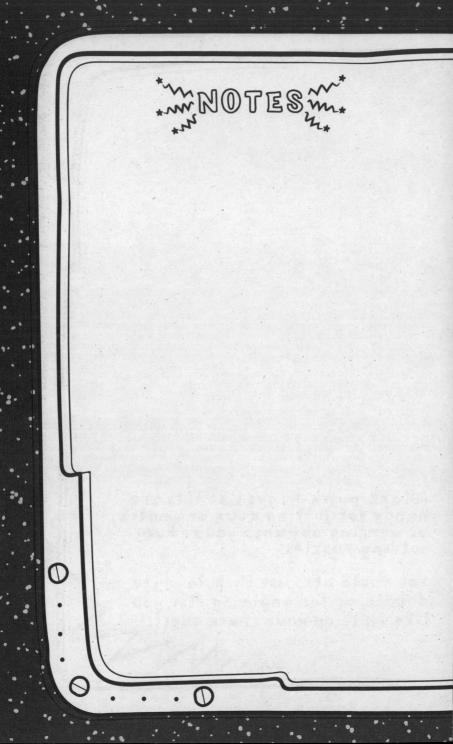

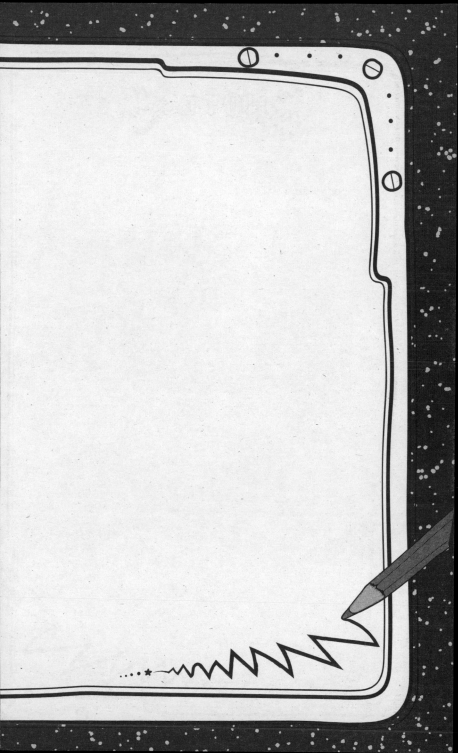

NOTES